Eva Wilder (McGlasson) Brodhead

Ministers of Grace

A Novelette

Eva Wilder (McGlasson) Brodhead

Ministers of Grace
A Novelette

ISBN/EAN: 9783337029715

Printed in Europe, USA, Canada, Australia, Japan

Cover: Foto ©Thomas Meinert / pixelio.de

More available books at **www.hansebooks.com**

MINISTERS OF GRACE

A Novelette

BY

EVA WILDER McGLASSON
AUTHOR OF
"DIANA'S LIVERY" "AN EARTHLY PARAGON" ETC.

ILLUSTRATED

NEW YORK
HARPER & BROTHERS PUBLISHERS
1894

ILLUSTRATIONS

MINISTERS OF GRACE

I

THE Syrian peddler wore a black skull-cap heavily braided. About his spare waist was buttoned a sort of cloth skirt, the wide flare of which accented the slightness of his figure. He had, indeed, so Wade decided, the lines of an ancient Egyptian, as shown in the vivacious mural sketches of Theban times. His finely impressed features were of a rich bronze tone, his mellow, appealing eyes very dark. As he lifted from his linen pack and flung before the women on the hotel steps a strip of crimson silk, or a gold-wrought tissue of white, a kind of alien grace and distinction disclosed themselves in his motions.

"Cheap!" he repeated, with plaintive persistence, gazing up from his kneeling posture

1

into the faces of the little throng. These faces, set off against the antique racial implication of his own sharp, swart visage, looked queerly commonplace in their bluntness of feature, freshness of color, heaviness of muscle. They were good-humored faces enough—such kind, broad, unspeculative faces as are by no means unusual; but as Wade regarded them from the east end of the porch, where he sat by himself, he had a little sense of amusement at the supremacy of his own new and prosperous country, as expressed in the portly condescension of these middle-aged countenances.

Some of the women turned over the delicate Eastern stuffs with disdaining hands. They tried on the silk shawls and weighed the fringes with calculating fingers. Generally they said, " Too dear, Marco," speaking very loudly, as to a deaf man. And while they haggled over his goods the vender of silks knelt at their feet, with his slender brown hands pathetically clasped, and his picturesque profile imploringly raised.

" What you give?" he pleaded, servilely. Behind him was a scenic background of

flawless summer sky and bright blue sea.
Faint garlands of smoke from an unseen vessel rose beyond the reach of sun - flecked
water. A schooner, with every inch of canvas out, slipped along the offing. Arc-lamps,
poles, webs of wire, a pausing trolley-car, and
the fretted roofs of a group of bath - houses
rose dark and clear upon the blending reach
of sea and heaven. Flags curled blithely
from hotel tops ; peaks, turrets, airy porches
stretched away in a dazzling freshness of new
paint; a fountain flung crystal threads above
its cupid-clasped basin in the green ribbon
of park fronting the Dorsheimer Arms.

The veranda of this house, unpeopled except for Wade and the group on the steps,
was set along its expanse with any number
of slim, pale - green pillars. Below a scroll-
sawed roof, scooped out in shallow arches,
heavy arm-chairs were sociably ranged, thick-
ening towards the west end, on which the
windows of the dance-hall gave. The other
end faced the ocean, which, like a gleaming
sword, flashed across the end of the street.

Wade, as he sat here, staring seaward,
found himself vaguely disturbed by the jab-

ber of the bargainers. There was, indeed, a mixture of noises this morning. A brass-band sent fitful screams of waltz music up from the beach, and somewhere nearer a cornet rasped inharmoniously. Children were running about the upper porches, and the gay laughter of some passing girls mingled strangely with the solemn murmur of the surf. It was noisy. And distinctly he had less tolerance for Hildreth Beach than he had found it easy in other days to command— had Wade.

He could plainly remember liking it immensely when, at odd times in the past ten years, the press of newspaper work permitted him to run down for a sniff of salt air and a day or so of such distractions as the big, heavily frivolous summer city had to offer. His nerves, he reminded himself, had perhaps been steadier during these former visits, and not, as at present, lax from an attack of fever. Perhaps when the salt sea should have wrought upon him for a week or two the old contentment would return? Yet, notwithstanding this possibility, Wade grew uncomfortably pensive over his sudden feeling of personal indifference. If he went on losing interest in things at this rate, and finding only annoyance in what had once given pleasure, what would life be in another decade, when he should face the windy side of forty? It was a very pretty question. Decidedly, since Hildreth affected him after a new order, he must have changed greatly. For Hildreth itself was practically unchangeable, having as patrons the sort of folk who maintain humanity's averages — a class too simple and primitive ever to vary much.

This slip of the coast was everywhere recognized as the junketing-ground of the masses. The kindly determined people who swarmed here in summer, to the number of tens of thousands, represented the great conservative, solidly respectable middle classes of the country—so far, indeed, as a republic may have such a class, or any class. They would have referred to themselves with pride as plain people. That they made little pretension to fashion was rather a vaunt with them. Of arts, letters, and philosophies they held large general views. They stood sound in the creeds of their respective churches, and had

correct ideas concerning American greatness.
They were apt, like folk of a more analytic
turn, to rate each other according to the tab-
ulation of Bradstreet. In fine, they abided
in a broad, unspeculative optimism and the
traditions of their rearing, believing happiness to be humanity's right, and mid-day the
best time for dinner.

And as they had a wholesome horror of the
silence and solitude that are dear to brain-
sick mystics, they adored Hildreth Beach,
which had short shrift for either—that is, in
the season. It was quiet enough at Hildreth
during the greater part of the year. But
though the peerless beach, the strong, sweet
air, the fir-groves and little lakes and stray
brooks and other merely natural aspects were
probably quite as charming then as at the
season's height, there was, of course, upon
them all the inevitable dulness which a lack
of engaging pastimes produces. It was only
in midsummer that the steam-launch and ob-
servation-wheel and toboggan-slide operated
with an accompaniment of brass-bands and
nightly hops and blazing electricity and im-
penetrable crowds. So, naturally enough ev-

cry one came at the same time, while these attractions were in full swing — every one who cared for amusement.

Incidentally many came for the bathing. The surf at Hildreth was incomparable, and a thought of the flat shelves of sand and creaming breakers reinvigorated Wade's mind. He rose, and, pocketing his thumbs, took in the powdery fling of the surge. He was a slight young man, who looked as if he might stand straighter if he had any object in it. There was a lot of heavy hair parted across the middle of his head and flattened down above the ears. He seemed of a whimsical habit of mind; there was a slow gleam in his brown eyes; his scrap of mustache twisted, too, as if used to the drag of a humorous lip muscle.

"The noise, the bustle, is just what I need," he assured himself, with the hopeful sense of one who has possessed, and perhaps still at heart possesses, that vast relish for life which is the gracious endowment of ordinary folk. "I'm not here to think, but to avoid thinking." And by a natural transition, at which he smiled, he found himself adding,

"I wonder where Gracie is? She's the card when a fellow's threatened with a fit of meditation!"

Wherewith he strolled towards the door of the office, on the sill of which the clerk, a stately-appearing young man, stood screwing the head on a fountain-pen.

"Miss Gayle about?" asked Wade.

"Bathing," said the clerk, succinctly. "Nice little lady, that. Awful fond of her mother, isn't she?" He glanced towards a small elderly woman who stood near the peddler, idly turning the large ruby ring on her spare, toil-worn finger.

"Very," agreed Wade, also bestowing a glance upon Miss Gayle's mother, who, with her wrinkled face, her knobbed gray hair, and honest, hard-working air, smiled back at the young man.

"A nice little lady," repeated the clerk, shaking the pen. "And popular! She gets everything that strikes the place. As her mother would say, 'She's a witch, soir, so she is, don't ye know? Arrah, there's danger in her eye! But nobody has the betther daughter, praise be to God!'" He broke off

in a decent attempt at Irish, and said, "She's
coming up the street now—three chaps with
her, too!"

It was round about the hour of noon, and
people were beginning to come up from the
beach. Some of them carried dripping garments knotted in bath towels. Now and then
a woman passed with unbound hair in wet
ropes about her shoulders. Men in summer
flannels joined infrequently in the throng.
The male element was less noticeably lacking at Hildreth than at other watering-places;
but even here it was in distinct minority, and
the sight of a girl attended by three young
men was remarkable enough to win the second glance.

She was a little thing—this Miss Gayle—
with a straight, alert figure, the motions of
which, as she walked, bore out the pert au-
dacity of her small Hibernic face. Her short
hair, crisp with the persuasive touch of hot
irons, relieved the clear red and white of a
skin in which a sort of waxen opacity was
evident. There was shrewdness in the black-
lashed, pale-blue eyes, impudence in the tilt-
ed nose, genuine geniality of temperament in

the girl's full lips. In a trim blue gown, with conspicuous anchors of white on the wide collar, in sailor hat, white gloves, and impossible-looking canvas boots, she appeared the apotheosis of a type common to the Irish tenement-house quarter of the city.

"Your chariot-wheels clank loudly this morning," said Wade, as the girl ran up the steps. She shot back a glance at her departing escort and laughed.

"Those boys?" she said. "The truth is, I'm finding things slow." And she added, as she dropped into a chair, "Very slow, indeed."

"With three adorers? I say nothing of myself, being no squire of dames. I realize that I may never hope to impress that flexible heart which—"

"Oh, bother!" said the other, fanning herself with her hat. "Sometimes I don't mind your chaff; but sometimes it don't strike me just right. This is one of the times."

"When you are cooler, you'll regret this harshness, Gracie." She made a little gesture of impatience.

"I'm not harsh; I'm only serious. It don't

sit well on you, that flirtatious sort of way
you drop into once in a while. You know
what I think of you. No—stop it! I'm not
joking. You know I like you; but not *that*
way any more than you do me. When it
comes to a real Simon-pure friendship, Selby
Wade, you'll find me right on time; that's
straight goods—sure. My heart may be—
what was it?—flexible. It may be flexible,
but I haven't forgot that write-up you gave
me two years ago. I hadn't caught on at all
up to that time. The public needed some
one to tell 'em I could dance just as well as
these Spanish señoritas they were raving
over—and you told 'em. I tell you—take
me up one side and down the other—I'm
not the crying kind; but when I read the
paper that day, and saw what a send-off
you'd given me, I keeled right over—yes,
I did; I wept like an infant; and so did
mom." She caught her breath in excited re-
membrance.

"I appreciated it," she continued. "It
came straight, it did. I had no pull with
the paper; I didn't even know who wrote
the story till I went and asked. And I

hadn't met so much kindness that I was used to it—I had not. I'm not ashamed to say I've worked my way up. I've told you how poor we were, mom and me. It wasn't much worse after my father died. He was a laboring man, and he drank, and we got along about as well without him. Mom worked out by the day and sent me to school, and when I was fifteen I got a place in the chorus. And I found I could sing a little, and I learned to dance. I stopped being Mamie Riley, and started out as Grace Gayle. I worked like a slave; and then all at once I caught the public. I'm right in with luck now—can sing where I please. And in a year or so I'm going across; and I'll do an American dance, with the colors wrapped round me; and they'll think it's national and all that; and when I come back to the land of the free, I will own it—see? They don't know a good thing here till some other country points it out."

"They've recognized you without transatlantic aid."

"Oh, their patriotism was roused when they had me described to 'em as a scrap of

American grit bucking against foreign powers! They're for protecting home industries every time. But I know 'em; and I don't expect to take 'em by storm till I come back with the foreign stamp on my label!"

The porch was now thronged. Girls in outing apparel chattered in the wide doorway of the office, paying court to a stripling or so, whose cigarette smoke curled thinly about the huddle of heads. Portly women filled the arm-chairs, and a few elderly men, with feet on the porch-rail, discussed the temperature of the water.

In the office itself, a square room overlooked by a spiral stairway, a compact group of girls were studying the register. The clerk was accepting a cigar from a pompous gentleman whose face shone rubicund from below his high silk hat. There was a little movement about the door. People began to rise from the arm-chairs, and Miss Gayle, lazily following this example, said: " I see it's dinner-time. Let's go in." She was looking beyond Wade into the sunny street, and her face presently assumed an expression of mild curiosity.

"Do you know who those people are?"
she asked, nodding roadward. "Queer out-
fit, isn't it? They only came yesterday. I
noticed 'em at supper. The girl struck me
kind of odd—like a frost-bitten flower, stiff
and cold."

Just below the porch a slight young person in a straight black frock, and with her
face hid in the flap of a wide white hat, was
coming up the cement walk, pushing before
her a wheeled chair. Over the back of this
a faded shepherd's plaid trailed, against which
leaned the head of a feeble-looking old man.
His wasted shape was hung in ministerial
broadcloth, and over his breast flared two
points of rough, silvery beard, matching in
hue the straggling locks in his neck. He
clutched at the chair-arms in a strange in-
tensity of grasp, which had something in
common with the meditative fixity of his
deep-set eyes. Neither twinkling fountain
nor flowery park nor thronged porch appeared to engage him. The whole specula-
tion of his face — perpendicular of brow,
beaked of nose, fierce of eye — seemed with-
drawn to inner sources of cheerless thought.

As the chair was drawn up at the base of the hotel steps he started.

" We are back, then, Elizabeth ?" he asked, in a perfunctory way, as if he cared little where he might be.

The young woman had come round to his side.

" Yes, father," she said. He lifted himself, and thrust one spare leg over the chair's edge. She was bending over him, and he had laid his hand upon her arm, struggling half erect. The effort seemed too much for his strength.

" I'm spent indeed," he muttered, sinking back—"a land laid waste."

Wade had started forward, treading as he went upon the Syrian's stuffs. He said, " Let me help you ;" and so drew the shrunken figure up from the low seat.

" Sir," declared the old man, with austere dignity, " your aid was most timely. I thank you."

" We thank you," echoed the girl, in a remote sort of voice.

" It was nothing," said Wade, bowing to her and noticing that her face was pale and soft of feature, with almost colorless lips, and dark, abstracted eyes. The young man took in these details indefinitely, being the more aware of the girl's expression of reserve, which was so marked as to give him a feeling of strangeness and curiosity.

II

"Some one told them we were quiet," said the clerk, smiling somewhat — "some one who'd been here long ago when Maynor had the place and put out the lights at ten and had cold dinners on Sunday." He paused to take a brass-hung key from a young woman. Then he turned again to Wade, who was leaning over the register, and added, "Things are very different since Dorsheimer took the house. Whatever else we are or are not, we're lively."

"There's no doubt about that," echoed Wade, feelingly. He had his eye on a feebly scrawled entry which read: "Rev. Thomas Ruley and daughter, High Ripple, Indiana," and as he read it he wondered that a man at once old and ill and a preacher should have elected to come to such a place as the Dorsheimer Arms.

For the Dorsheimer Arms, as the clerk had

2

said, was very lively indeed. It had dancing by night and music at all times, and its parlors, porches, and corridors were constantly thronged with gay multitudes. It was only in the reading-room, a somewhat barren department off the dance-hall, that quietude and seclusion ever held sway. For the Hildreth public was not given to wasting its holiday time over fresh or musty folios, and books were indeed so rare a sight in the hands of Hildreth sojourners that Wade, coming into the unfrequented reading-room upon a certain occasion not long after his chat with the clerk, was something surprised to see a burly black volume in the hand of a man near the window.

This person, turning at Wade's step, peered with poring eyes, and, recognizing the young man, held out a knotted hand.

"You are looking better to-day," said Wade, with resolute cheerfulness. The old preacher's face gloomed over, and he dragged his ragged beard together with bony fingers.

"I notice little change," he demurred. "The noise irritates me. In truth, I am un-

"REV. THOMAS RULEY AND DAUGHTER, HIGH RIPPLE,
INDIANA"

fit for such sights and sounds as prevail
here, having long been possessed of a pining
sickness." His voice was slightly nasal, with
an accent that lingered in the style of the
country orator upon unimportant but regu-
larly recurring syllables. It had also a singular depth, a sort of passionate undertone.
And as he talked he flung his hands out in
sweeping gestures, over-fluent, almost melo-
dramatic.

" We little expected to find ourselves in a
house overrun with the godless hordes of fashion," he went on. " It seems that the place
was very different some years since, when my
friend Amos Fitch, of High Ripple, spent
two days here. My daughter wishes to find
a quieter place, but I cannot see our way
clear. Our arrangements were for a certain
period, and I point out to her how ill a
break of contract would beseem us. Elizabeth is scrupulously conscientious. I have
rarely seen a more lovely nature. But in
matters of business I regret to say she is not
so—I might say, so far-sighted as I would
wish."

He sighed deeply as he thumbed his big

book. In a moment he added that his daughter had yielded to his views. "But she feels it—she feels it sorely that I should be disturbed by anything, for she persuaded me to come here against my better judgment. The doctor advocated sea-air for me. But I knew that my infirmity was not to be reached, or, I may say, ameliorated. And I realized the folly of wasting our limited substance in the pursuit of the health I should never regain. Elizabeth, however — I am weak, very weak in those small hands of hers—this child of my old age, left motherless in her babyhood. And I gave in—I gave in! But in the presence of such folly and irreverence as reign here in this mere place of pleasure I am greatly cast down. I say little to Elizabeth, but I have continual heaviness of heart." He shut his eyes, as one who sees his Nineveh given to the owls and bats.

When he opened them it was with a start. The strains of a *gavotte* had begun to crash out in the dance-hall, and at the first note a lot of young folk came trooping down the porch. One girl, glancing into the reading-room, caught sight of Wade, and paused on the threshold of the long window to do him a fine courtesy.

It was Miss Gayle who thus airily plucked back her blue skirts, revealing the trimmest of ankles, the highest of heels, the whitest of lace petticoat-frills. Tossing her dark curls, and blowing a coquettish stage-kiss from her finger-tips, she wheeled round and away.

The eyes of the Rev. Mr. Ruley rested on her with austere reprobation.

"A daughter of Heth," he said, deeply, waving off the iniquitous vision with a stern hand — "such as walk with outstretched necks, mincing as they go. I have observed this misguided young woman before. She represents, I am told, that most debasing of modern institutions, the stage."

"She's an actress, but—"

"So I understood. I can but trust that my Elizabeth will not be forced by the demands of courtesy into any knowledge of her."

Wade's brow protested a little.

"Miss Gayle is a wonderfully self-respecting little girl," he insisted. "Whatever chance at life she's had she's made for herself.

She's a flower of the slums—the offshoot of poverty and ignorance. She's worked hard to make a career, has Gracie. And I can't see that it could possibly debase any one to witness the charming and modest dances she is noted for."

"I will not further enunciate my views on the particular profession to which this young person belongs," formally declared the other, "but I may say that I do not approve of the reprehensible modern spirit which leads women to desire careers of any sort." He pointed a denunciative finger. "The distaff is the symbol of the truest womanhood. To mind the house, tend the sick, rear children— these are its blessed privileges. But," cried Mr. Ruley, waxing hot, "when women forswear the hearth for the lancet, the law, the pen—when they even lift in the sanctuary itself those voices that were given them to soothe the suckling at their breasts— then, sir—then!—as a stanch upholder of pure and primitive doctrine, I declare against them!"

"Well," smiled Wade, "why not let them try their hand?—they're bound to, anyhow!

And the success of the most illustrious won't change the features of ordinary men's ideal woman—the white lily of seclusion, the soft-eyed, home-keeping creature whose unambitious brows are forever bent on a long white seam."

"I agree with you entirely!" cried Mr. Ruley, taking this seriously. "My Elizabeth, now—my own daughter—is bread-winner for both of us. But amid my desolation—for I bear, sir, the weight of a bitter disappointment—it is much of a comfort to me that her position is a sheltered one. She has been, since she left school three or four years since, companion to a former member of my congregation, now a wealthy Chicago woman. Of course it keeps us apart, for I remain at High Ripple, the scene of my labor and my great trial. But I am used to His rods, and I have the consolation of knowing that Bessie is lovingly regarded and protected. And her service permits her to spend some weeks of the summer with me."

His strident tones rang loud, for the music had stopped. Other voices sounded near by as a party of girls gathered in the ball-room door. The old man rose stiffly; he had descried his daughter coming across the long room, and as she approached, he said, "I have missed you, Elizabeth."

"I was helping to move our things, father," she said, giving Wade a small, sedate nod. "They've found us quieter rooms." She glanced curiously towards the buxom, beribboned girls in the doorway—herself a strange unit of contrast with them, in her sober gown, her quaintly braided black hair, her whiteness, slightness, and chill constraint.

"She looks as hard and as fragile as a scrap of carved ivory — this stand-offish young person," thought Wade. But just then, as she bent to speak to her father, the shadow of a smile flickered over her face, so softening it that the young man changed his figure.

"Set off against those blooming creatures yonder," he said to himself, "she is like a sprig of mignonette in a bunch of cabbage-roses."

The girls he thus massed in a metaphor not altogether flattering seemed to be holding a whispered consultation. Then one of them stepped forward, and Wade, seeing that it was Grace Gayle, held himself to witness her intent.

"Mr. Wade," she said, "introduce me to Mr. and Miss Ruley. You see I know your names! I hope you're getting better, Mr. Ruley. You seemed pretty weak the other day. I tell you it's awful—that limber feeling in the knees! I've had it. Only mine came from stage-fright." She turned graciously to Elizabeth and said, "You don't seem to know any one here, so I just told the girls I was going to come right up and speak to you. I told 'em I wasn't going to stand on ceremony; I'm never stiff in a place like this. I liked the looks of you, and I told 'em I was going to see that you had a rattling good time this summer. That's how I am."

Miss Ruley regarded her with a little, impassive smile. For all her severe attire her face looked almost childlike beside the shrewd alertness of Grace's small features.

"You are very good," she said, in a guarded sort of voice—"very good indeed." And then she moved away—she and her father—across the bare expanse of floor.

Grace's face twisted.

"I didn't seem to strike 'em just right," she admitted. "But say, I know what was wrong: they were a little afraid of me because I'm an actress, and successful, and all that! The old man probably thinks I've a silly prejudice against preachers. Now I haven't — not a bit. You tell him, won't you, Mr. Wade, that I'm not at all stuck-up, or bigoted, or anything. Tell him I haven't a thing against religion. Because I want to get on with the daughter. I'm sorry for the poor little soul. I bet she never had a bit of fun since the day she was born. She's a little cool, and my spine kind of froze when she turned her big, innocent eyes on me. But she'll like me when she knows me," added Grace, complacently. She smiled as she turned away. And Wade smiled also, as he remembered the impressive stateliness of the small figure in the black frock which had just swept through the doorway.

III

A RUSSET-TONED dusk was settling thickly
on the ocean. From its farthest brown density breakers levelled themselves landward
in hollow, granite-like plates. Stars, muffled
in mist, shone far and faint. Out on the flat
reach of water a lighted steamer moved slow-
ly through the fog, looking not unlike a great
phosphorescent fish with a dorsal fin of lu-
minous silver. The color of the pale young
moon in the southern sky seemed a wan reflex of a sunset still wrapping the west in
vague primrose. Lances of light moment-
ly darted from hotel windows and porches,
matching in hue the sky's low saffron, and
making the dark buildings lifted against it
look like mere walls, through crevices of
which the after-glow poured.

Above the foam-streaked sands the beach-
walk stretched long and narrow, jotted at in-
tervals with prim little benches and large and

small pavilions. Being Saturday night, there
was more than the usual throng gathering
for the evening promenade, and sounds of
talk and laughter rang insistently above the
echo of the surf and the intermittent strains
of a band of music somewhere down the
beach. Men in unwonted numbers strolled
along the lifted planks at the sea's verge,
generally smoking as they loitered onward,
and having upon them a loose and easy air
as of briefly-dismissed business worries and
relaxed social conventions.

Everywhere in street and veranda were
noise and bustle and pressing crowds. The
office of the Dorsheimer Arms was thronged
to the doors. A large placard on the clerk's
desk announced a " Full-dress Hop," and the
notable absence from view of young women
seemed to indicate special toilet-making in
honor of the occasion.

Wade, leaning against a porch pillar, was
talking to a man with whom he had a casual
acquaintance—a man whose presence at Hildreth was directly owing to Miss Gayle. It
was not, however, as a suitor to the young
woman that Mr. Bailey had come to the

beach, unless, incidentally, love, as a divert-
ing but inconsequent feature of life, should
develop from the purely business arrangements he was seeking.

" He's going to take out 'The King's Jest-
ers,'" Grace had told Wade. "But I don't
think I'll sign with him. I'm a big feature
now, and I don't have to leave town. He's
made me good offers, Bailey has, and I like
him first-rate ; he's a rattling manager. Just
made Daisy Higby—a pretty little dancer,
though not original at all. I guess he's been
everything—from a district messenger-boy to
a government detective. He knows the ropes,
and he'd push me. But I'm not spoiling for
the circuit. New York's good enough for
me."

Mr. Bailey, perhaps with a sustaining be-
lief in his persuasive powers, had just stated
to Wade his design of " putting in " a couple
of weeks at Hildreth.

" I'd like to make terms with Gracie," he
owned. "She isn't as handsome as some,
and her voice is n. g. But she's got a trick
with a house — magnetism, maybe. She's
dead sure of a call when the star hasn't

caught on a little." Bailey had about him a sort of boyish candor which people usually found rather winning. He was slim and undersized, with a face whose mild ingenuousness sheathed an expression as keen as a blade. There was a dimple in his chin. He had blue eyes, and a mustache as yellow as the breast of a meadow-lark. But the frankness of his glance held a furtive element; an air of the hoodlum clung to him; his mental outlook seemed cunning rather than intelligent. The New York streets had been Bailey's teachers in the game of life, and if he knew how to load the dice it was perhaps not altogether odd.

As the two men elbowed their way across the porch and strolled seaward they reviewed Miss Gayle's capabilities and discussed the theatrical outlook generally.

"We've lost our best," said Wade, as they came to the north end of the walk, always comparatively free of strollers because distant from the band-stands, "and, so far as I know, there is no sign of any superlative talent among our younger players. Grace, facility, intelligence, and taste we have in abun-

dance, but the mantle of Booth, Barrett, or
McCullough has fallen on no one's shoulders. Well, perhaps the question of purely
original genius is less a matter of supply than
of demand! It's the Gracie Gayle sort of
thing that people care for nowadays."

"It's the age of *vaudeville*."

"Yes; of the *pirouette*. It's rose-wreaths,
not bay, that catch us. And, by gad! if we
consent to take anything seriously it's got to
be uncommon, with a psychological twist in
the stuff: Ibsen, and those other fellows—
Maeterlinck, Sudermann, Streiedberg."

"Oh, taste changes," debated the other,
leaning on one of the damp benches, and
watching the cliffy rise of the waxing breakers. "But I believe there's always a steady
interest in the old legitimate plays—down
under the passing notion for farce and philosophy, I mean. Let a man do Hamlet well,
and he'll find a public any time. By-the-bye,
speaking of Hamlet, have you ever seen young
Vercamp do the gloomy Dane?"

"Vercamp?"

"I guess he's never showed in the East;
but he's got a future, that chap. Only twenty

or so ; chock-full of talent. I've my eye on
him. He's a little raw yet, but coming right
up. Oh, I tell you, we've got stuff in this
country! There's the Averne girl, too. I
saw her play Juliet a year ago in a hole of a
Missouri town. Lank, unformed, scared-look-
ing thing ; but fire? Jove! She'll never
catch on, though, till she's pushed. I tell
you," cried Bailey, lashing the darkness with
the butt of a cigarette, "Rachel wouldn't draw
in these times without paper and pushing."

The peals of a three-piece band broke on
their ears while they were yet a long way
from the Dorsheimer Arms. Through the
long windows of the dance-hall the young
men could see a maze of moving figures. People sat thick about the walls and thronged
the thresholds. The windows facing the
court-yard were black with the visages of the
servants of the house looking in upon the
dancers.

Most of the women were in evening-gowns.
Among the men an occasional dress-suit re-
vealed itself, but for the greater part tweeds
and flannels prevailed. The girls seemed generally young and good-looking, with a predis-

position to overreach their partners in weight and robustness, for the men were notably pale and thin. Their lack of brawn and buoyancy suggested long hours in great furnace-heated shops or close offices.

This same phenomenon of comparison presented itself in the older folk, complacently observing their sons and daughters circle round the waxed floor. Whether the women had paid court to fashion in crimping their gray locks and cramping their ample waists, or whether they abided in the traditions of a youth which had gone decent in smooth hair and plain gowns, all had a ponderous well-fed aspect, as set off against the leanness of the elderly men.

" Fine figures of girls," commented Bailey.

"M—yes. I shouldn't wonder if the woman's question would eventually become a mere matter of the survival of the fittest; for, gad! it looks as if a few ages more would eliminate men entirely from the social equation of the masses." He broke off to address Gracie Gayle, who floated towards them in an interval of the music.

" Of course you want to dance with me ?"

3

she signified, tilting forward on her scarlet heels.

"I long, but forbear," said Wade, lazily. "I bless thee, yet renounce thee to thy face." Yet Grace, frilled round in flimsy scarlet, and with a red rose coquetting it behind one ear, was not without a charm of her own. She had the air and stature of a child, but in her clear eyes was the piquancy of a deeper knowledge than sheltered women have. It gave Wade something like a twitch of the heart, a sentiment both pitiful and admiring, to think of the paths through which those small feet had marched so securely.

He watched Bailey move away with her. There was an initiatory rasp of a violin, and Wade, with the idea of a solitary, pensive cigar, made way through the packed chairs and pushed towards the remote, unthronged end of the gallery.

As he approached this quiet spot, however, the violent flickering of the big arc-light over the curb pointed the fact of a chair drawn up in the very situation he had figured. He was almost upon it before he saw that a woman was sitting there with her chin in her hand

"A CHAIR DRAWN UP IN THE VERY SITUATION HE
HAD FIGURED"

and with her eyes set on the fog trailing past the high globe of the electric lamp.

At Wade's approach she turned with a decided start, and, recognizing him, said, " Oh !" and sank back as with a sort of relief.

"You are not dancing," said Wade, whose acquaintance with Mr. Ruley's young daughter was still of a limited nature.

" I—a preacher's child ?"

" Oh !" laughed Wade, encouraged by her own smile. " But the dance may express anything—grief, triumph, joy, even religious ecstasy." The ball-room music struck through this idea, compacting itself with the young man's sense of the salt air straying palpably across his face. Whatever those strains might mean to young blood, Wade reflected that they had probably sent Mr. Ruley to bed filled with an anguished consciousness of desperate iniquity on the part of the " godless hordes of fashion " he figured as making up the Hildreth throngs.

" Papa sees people as weak and sinful," said Elizabeth Ruley, sighing a little. "And he dislikes everything which identifies itself with the folly of a fallen race. You see ?"

" Er—yes."

" It seems terrible to him that people on the brink of—well of perdition—should disport themselves with careless gayety. He has always been like one crying in a wilderness of apathy and unconcern. Poor papa !" She broke off and fastened a questioning eye on Wade. " He's told you, hasn't he, about his trouble with the church at home ?"

" About their asking him—"

" To resign — yes. That was a terrible time. He had preached there so long ! I don't think he ever suspected that they were tired of him and his ways. And indeed there were those who stood by him. But a younger generation had come up—a generation demanding revised scriptures and changed creeds and general good cheer from the sacramental cup. They wanted a sparkling, enlivening vintage instead of the drink my father gave them. They didn't want to hear about their shortcomings, or the insecurity and bitterness of life. They said that papa preached over their heads and didn't attract the young people, and they sent a committee to ask him to give up the charge.

Oh, it was terrible! Their dissatisfaction was like a thunder-bolt to papa. I cannot repeat all he said to them in his last sermon. But he denounced them without measure, and he never entered the pulpit again, nor has he ever been the same since. He shut himself for three days in his study, and would not speak even to me. And when he finally tottered out he looked like a man who has got his death-blow—though that was four years since."

She paused with a tremor in her soft voice. The night wind chopped round the porch end with a mournful cry. The fog, slipping past the high globe, took the likeness of fleeting figures. It seemed as if the darkness were full of homeless sprites, which, as they sped past the globe of flame, shivered closer to it for the warmth and light.

Sitting in the hazy shadows Elizabeth Ruley herself looked hardly real, so white and slight she seemed in her black garments. The weight which her father bore had crushed her also. She seemed the merest shadow of girlhood, a passive, cloistral sort of creature, unused to the sun, and altogether too spiritless to resent the unnatural gloom in which she dwelt.

Two people were coming down the porch.

"Feel how damp my hair is!" cried one of them, a girl, shaking her brine-touched curls. "It'll be straight as a poker before I can turn round." She peered down the veranda, and, seeing Wade, tripped towards him, holding up her scarlet ruffles. Seeing that he was not alone she drew wide eyes and pointed a small finger.

"So!" she said. "You are having it all to yourself down there."

"I was just going in," the other woman said, smiling a little as she rose. "If you will excuse me," she added, to Wade. He felt a vivid sense of resentment at Gracie for disturbing a talk which had, at least, held a certain element of sympathy. But Gracie herself seemed unaware of this. She perched on the low porch-rail beside him, with her frills drawn up, her red heels swinging, her hair loosening in great waves as the dampness brushed over it. The whole salt-smelling darkness appeared as if disturbed by her frivolous presence. Wade rose irritably, observing the slight, dark-gowned figure of Elizabeth Ruley pausing just then at the turn of the circling stair. She had evidently forgotten her room-key, and came down to get it from the clerk.

" I think she likes me better than she did at first," Gracie was saying. " I knew I'd win if I played long enough on one color !" Her tone rang complacently in Wade's ear as he moved towards the office door. Elizabeth had turned again to the stairway, but Wade was withheld from noticing her further by a sudden recognition of the fact that Bailey, standing just in the embrasure of the door, had his ingenuous eyes fixed intently on the ascending figure of Mr. Ruley's daughter. Wade stepped over the threshold. As he did so Bailey withdrew his gaze and turned rather quickly.

" Wade," he said, shortly, " you were talking to her out there. Who is she?—that girl !"

IV

WADE regarded his questioner with distinct coldness.

"That is Miss Ruley," he said, briefly.

"Miss Ruley?"

"Miss Ruley. You'll find my statement corroborated in the register." And remembering the scrawling entry which had afforded him the information which Bailey was now seeking, he murmured, "'The Rev. Thomas Ruley and daughter, High Ripple, Indiana.'"

"Thanks," said Bailey, staring a little.

His voice had lapsed to an accent of indifference. Having lighted a cigarette he turned away. Wade looked after him thoughtfully, being somewhat amused at the briefly vivid character of the young man's interest in Elizabeth Ruley. It seemed, as days went on, that this interest had been, indeed, of a momentary nature, for Bailey made no effort

at seeking any acquaintance with the young
woman in question, though the exigencies of
the hotel porch and the considerate offices of
Miss Gayle forced him into such social knowledge of the preacher's daughter as an intro-
duction is supposed to effect.

These same days cast Wade considerably
with the Ruleys. Some latent fibre of the
old man's being responded to the other's
quiet whimsicality. Wade was wise enough
never to combat any of the preacher's pronounced and contorted views, and as a con-
sequence the relations between them came to
be of a pleasant and friendly sort.

Everything at Hildreth wore a gentle aspect. The sea was a bland sheet of milky
green, whose shallow breakers wreathed the
sands in blossomy white; the skies hung
placid; the very multitudes seemed to im-
bibe a certain languid quietude from the midsummer serenity.

Of mornings every one went bathing, and
the pole-spiked surf resembled a great human
brew, bubbling up with heads and arms. At
a little distance the bathers lost all mortal
significance, seeming rather like the top twigs

of a submerged forest, peaking rough and
black through the circling waves. On the
warm sand under the biggest pavilion people squatted at ease, watching the antics of
the bathers. The number of these constantly
grew, as men and women in baggy blue flannels strolled seaward from the bath-houses.

Children with wood spades cast up frail
fortifications against the surf. They shouted
as they worked, and a small dog, digging in
the sand just beyond the usual station of Mr.
Ruley's chair, barked furiously at some im-
aginary quarry. Mr. Ruley spoke to him
twice in a mildly reproachful way, for the
shrill staccato barks made his ears tingle.
But the terrier kept on honey-combing the
beach with his sharp paws. His flanks shook,
his eyes bulged in an ecstasy of pursuit, and
he appeared unconscious of the gaunt figure
hard by, bent together under its plaid shawl,
and holding on its knee a package of small
leaflets.

Whenever any one strolled near his chair
Mr. Ruley held out one of the pamphlets.
No one refused the offering of the shaking
hand, and the old man's purblind gaze failed

to see, blowing airily along the sands, the
sheets so lately received of him with good-
natured indifference. Now and then one of
these printed squares, motionless in the wane
of the breeze, displayed a heading which ex-
horted, announced, or appealed. Oftener they
were trodden down by the feet of passers, or
were carried over the water, lifting and hurt-
ling along like callow gulls.

Wade, coming down the beach in bathing
apparel, paused beside the chair. Mr. Ruley
tremulously proffered a leaf bearing a pious
adjuration, but, recognizing the young man,
he laid the thing back and seemed to bright-
en up.

"I do not give these to you, a thinking
man," he explained. "They are for the careless. I doubt if one in a thousand reads or
heeds the admonition. But barren as my
ministry has been the habit of the sower
sticks with me, and, though I scatter seed
upon rock, I cannot withhold my hand."

A girl, screaming with laughter and spray-
ing the air with brine from her wet short
skirts, flew by, pursued by a brawny young
fellow. Children were wading in the low

shore-surf. Lovers mooned together on the
sea verge. Portly women gossiped on the
benches above the sand. Against all this
Mr. Ruley looked singularly lonely, and Wade
glanced about, wondering if Elizabeth were
not somewhere near.

"Elizabeth is walking with a friend of
ours," said the other, catching at Wade's
intent—"a friend from High Ripple, who
came rather unexpectedly this morning. A
young man "—he amplified, taking his usual
oratorical style, which reduced the single hear-
er to an indefinite part of a visionary throng
—"of much promise. A laborer like myself
in the Lord's vineyard, but blessed with fruit-
ful ingathering." He sighed and laid his
long arms over his breast. "You have heard
me speak of the Rev. Frederic Clinton Graham ?"

"Oh yes!" signified Wade, not altogether
charmed with this intelligence. He had
heard of the Rev. Mr. Graham, as he had
heard of many other features of High Ripple—of the old house in which the Ruleys
lived, the discovery of gas in the town's
outskirts, the worthy few who stood faithful

to their old pastor, and the new congregation which had ousted him.

Mr. Graham, as Wade remembered, did not belong to the ante-gas epoch. The drowsy village had become a bustling town before Mr. Ruley's young friend came to shed a genial influence upon it. For that Mr. Graham had extremely pleasing traits Wade could scarcely doubt, in view of the surprising fact that the man commanded the warmest affection not only of Mr. Ruley's former congregation, but also of Mr. Ruley himself.

Just in what sort he was regarded by Mr. Ruley's daughter Wade could only surmise. The mere circumstance of Graham's presence in Hildreth was suggestive of possibilities which Wade had not considered before, and the young man drew a grim smile as it came upon him that his own cordial intercourse with the Ruleys was likely to be disturbed by Graham's arrival.

At the consciousness that his face was taking on a sulky cast Wade straightened his shoulders. What difference did it make that a young woman whom he had known for several weeks was perhaps the sweetheart of a worthy Indiana clergyman? He, Wade, was not in love ; and, now that he came to think of it, he was glad that he was not. For, aside from the chance of a prior suitor, Wade declared to himself the connubial vista had no charms worth setting off against the easy-going privileges of bachelorhood — that is, for men of moderate finances. Domestic life in New York apartment-houses did not win upon Wade's fancy. These thousand-celled hives of the city's millions were most unattractive to him, and he cheerfully reconciled himself to the perpetual loneliness which has so placid and pleasant a face when examined by the heart-free.

Reverting to these early principles, Wade walked into the surf and dashed off, with a handful of brine, a half-formulated vision of Mr. Graham as a mild young man, whose conciliating chin sheered meekly into a white lawn tie.

"No doubt he's mighty at mothers' meeting, and waxes tearful over the babies he baptizes," thought Wade. "And Elizabeth is cut out for a preacher's wife—little, sweet, serious thing she is!"

That evening, as he came down to supper, he encountered Grace Gayle in the office. Grace wore a thoughtful air, and she drew Wade aside with an imperative nod.

"Do you know," she observed, gravely, "that you are not in it? Have you seen the new man? He's been with Miss Ruley all day."

"Alas, yes!" sighed Wade, elaborately. "I know that my goose is cooked. I've got a life-long sorrow to cherish, Gracie. I've always wanted something I could entirely devote myself to."

"Laugh it off as much as you please," scoffed Gracie, "but it won't take *me* in. I know something about men. None of 'em likes to take a back seat. It isn't human nature. So come off."

"What would you have me do—go about with a pale, disordered look?"

"I'd have you keep right to the front. This Graham's good-looking—splendid shoulders—looks like he might be a great centre-rush—but I believe you can beat his time. Take your hands out of your vest-pockets, and stop biting your mustache! Throw your shoulders back—"

" I stoop to conquer, Gracie."

" —and let him see that you're not going to be overlooked in the shuffle. I'd stay right with 'em all the time. That'll queer the whole business. He can't make love with you around."

She gave him a reassuring pat as she slipped away.

As Wade stood in the porchway after supper, and took critical stock of the man who sat talking with the Ruleys, he was aware of a surprised recognition of the justice of Miss Gayle's opinions. He was no ascetic stripling, this big fellow at Elizabeth's side. He had a shaven face of a cordial turn, thick, breezy hair, and a hearty laugh. Moreover, he wore a business-like suit of rough wool, and the hat on the floor near him was of white straw. There was a red flower in his button-hole. He was young and athletic, with nothing whatever about him intimative of stripes or fasting.

Mr. Ruley, catching Wade's eye, bent forward and summoned him. There was nothing then for the young man but to join the little group and extend a genial hand to the

person whom Mr. Ruley affectionately termed
his "own son in the faith." Presently he
was sitting with them as usual of evenings,
while the crowd surged by on its way to the
beach, and lights struck out of the twilight,
and music began to lilt up near and far.

" These thousands of human creatures, un-
deterred from their follies by the awful so-
lemnity of the great sea, afford an appalling
example of the blindness of such as are carnal
and sold unto sin," said Mr. Ruley. " You
must go down and observe the throng on the
beach, Frederic. The frivolity is, I may say,
more marked at evening than at other times.
For night brings thoughts of prayer and meditation to our hearts, and here the darkening
hours are given to unhallowed revelry."

Graham assented. Easy acquiescence appeared, indeed, to be his marked character-
istic.

" What's the use of setting yourself against
the big currents?" he inquired of Wade,
when their acquaintance had reached a standing of several days. "You don't accomplish
anything by it, except to get knocked ashore,
a mere bit of wreckage."

4

"Queer doctrine for one of your profession," Wade threw in. But Graham laughed his hearty, honest laugh.

"Bah!" he said. "There's no reason why a preacher shouldn't talk sense. In fact, he's *got* to talk it if he expects to reach people. They've ceased to care for rambling metaphysical dissertations. You've got to appeal to men's business as well as to their bosoms. These aren't visionary times." He added, in a moment, "Such as prevailed when ideas of special ordination were still active."

"Oh, then you don't hold for a chosen generation, a royal priesthood?"

"Me?—no. Personally I do not. I didn't go into the Church because I saw visions or heard the heathen clamoring for my aid. I took up theology—as perhaps others do—just as I would have taken up any profession. It's a respectable calling, and I had my living to make. I don't see that a fellow who accepts it in a business-like way is any less honest than one who is a bit exalted and yearns over humanity."

"Maybe not. But preaching don't pay very well, Graham. This is not the era when

prelates ' riot in ease and cumbrous wealth.'
A man's generally disinterested when he
dons the beretta. He has a right to be thought
so, anyhow."

" It all depends on his objectives. I admit
that the pulpit isn't specially lavish in finan-
cial returns; but, like literature, it has its com-
pensations. A clergyman has position. He
has also what is highly exceptional in the rush
of modern life—time to think, to plan, to live.
I took this into consideration. I wanted lei-
sure. I wanted a calling in which my knack
of speaking plainly and easily would count.
I had no pronounced convictions—few people have—concerning religious dogma. But
I got my finger on the pulse of the times
and found what the masses felt on these sub-
jects. And then I established myself on this
base, reflecting that it's well

> " ' When you censure the age
> To be cautious and sage.'

A preacher's function, as I see it, is merely
to direct the religious ceremonials of a
community. He's got to be up to date and
know the moral taste of the people. He must

feed them according to the demands of their palate, and not, for their own good even, force nauseous doctrine down their unwilling throats. Otherwise he'll find himself a failure — like our old friend yonder. He had passion and patience, and he wrought like a slave to cause his people to see the wisdom of so fashioning their lives as to merit heaven by making life a hell. They were not built on that plan, however!" The Rev. Mr. Graham paused to laugh again.

"I haven't half his powers," he went on; "but while he preached to empty pews, my church—which was also his—is jammed to the walls. My piety is of a gladsome order. I'm easy, colloquial, humane. By a continual rattling hail of sharp points—anecdotes, metaphors, allusions—I riddle the veil of apathy so apt to clog the Sabbath intelligence. I mix with folks socially. And when they have fairs and tableaux in the Sunday-school-room I smile and applaud instead of standing afar off and bitterly denouncing them for desecrating the sanctuary — as was Ruley's engaging habit."

"I can understand that you are popular,"

intimated Wade, conscious of a certain half-
amused distaste.

" Oh, I'm popular !" smiled Graham. " I'm
a power with the young men—the hardest
nuts a minister has to crack. I reach them
by carrying myself as one familiar in the past
with pleasant little vices, and not so far away
from those laxer times as to have forgotten
the taste of cakes and ale, or to have lost
sympathy with fellows whose business hasn't
forced them to a certain austerity of life.
I've a gentle scourge for the sinner's back.
What I can't uphold in way of social pastimes I leave alone." His voice had a tone
of simple good-nature, and Wade found himself liking this Timothy of the decadence,
however the young man's views went cross to
his own traditions of the priestly office.

Graham had a kind of primitive human
quality, which, being temperamental and irre-
spective of moral traits, must have attracted
both puritan and pagan. He and Wade took
many walks together. Sometimes they rolled
before them old Mr. Ruley's chair. Sometimes Elizabeth joined them, and her bearing, so far as Wade could see, put both

young men upon an equal footing of passive favor.

"To see her disturbed!" Wade sometimes said to himself, in view of the girl's passion-less calm. "Anger—anything—would be a relief. She seems utterly without emotional capacity, this agate-eyed young person. Yet we're generally hanging round her, I notice, Graham and I!"

One night as the three strolled towards the beach just on the edge of dark, they saw a great moon heaving its rosy shoulders above the rippling dove-hue of the ocean. Moment-ly the delicate pink of the rising sphere changed to a clearer red. Then a hint of orange dashed it, and suddenly the jagged sea appeared as if smitten across with a blazing sword—the sharp reflex of the lifting light. It was quiet, almost lonely, at the farthest end of the walk. Only the murmuring of the surf took the ear, as the rising tide nibbled with white teeth at the crusted sands. Against the faded western crimson sparks of white and amber flickered. A narrow lake to the left looked like a sprig of burnished coral under the sinking redness of the sky.

Graham, with his hat far back, and with a cheery light in his good-looking face, talked for the party. For Wade was in a pensive mood, and beside him Elizabeth walked in silence, looking far out at the water with eyes which held now, as ever, a teasing mystery of reticence.

Two men came in sight on the board promenade. Their figures were outlined in solitary distinction upon the tremulous ground of shining sea. One seemed to be a common-looking fellow in smart but cheap attire. The other, sauntering nearer, caught Wade's attention by reason of a certain Byronic affectation of languid cynicism. He had a dissipated pallor, a limp shirt-front, and longish black coat, which, as he walked, whipped about his knees. A general shabbiness hung over him. His hat was rakishly tipped, his oily hair worn rather long.

He came on with his companion, and threw a glance upon the people in the path. Suddenly Wade saw his pale face light up. The fellow paused as if startled, and then strode forward with a hand outstretched.

" *You* here?" he cried, in a tone of enthusiastic incredulity—"you here at the beach! I never dreamed you—" He broke off as if the mere delight of coming thus unexpectedly upon Elizabeth Ruley had quite robbed him of the power of speech.

Wade, pausing with the others, turned a surprised glance upon the girl beside him. It was a mistake, no doubt, this apparent recognition. But perhaps, after all, she knew the man—for she had stopped short in the way, and stood rigid, as if her joints went stiff with some most unwelcome sense. She seemed as if holding her breath, and her eyes were wide. Then something that was like a shiver went over her, and a hot red shook in her cheeks.

"How strange," she said, advancing a step to meet the man's reaching hand—"how strange to meet you here!" And turning to Wade and Graham, she added, "Mr. Wilmuth is an old—friend of mine. I should like to speak to him about something in which we are mutually interested—if you will walk on and let me catch up with you presently?"

V

THE two men thus admonished walked onward. A certain sense of strangeness hung in the moral atmosphere; but neither of them spoke of the matter. Graham's brow had, for a moment, a drawn sort of expression. Then as the refrain of a distant band wandered to his ears he began to hum the melody. Some girls with white scarfs on their heads passed by, casting gay glances at the young men, and Graham regarded them without clerical severity.

"I used to like girls like that—full of go and gayety—till I met Miss Ruley," he observed. "In fact, I was interested in her before I ever saw her, from hearing her father talk. As soon as I reached the town I heard of his troubles, and I went to see him. He rather took to me, strangely enough; and I learned of his daughter. He used to read me parts of her daily letters—faithful girl, that!

So I felt well acquainted with her when she came home in March. The old man gave down completely at that time, and she dropped everything and came to him. Of course, living as she does with a friend of the family, it was less difficult than it might have been in other circumstances."

Graham stopped to yawn and look round. Elizabeth was coming towards them. Her little light figure swept along the walk with diminutive dignity, and she was quite alone. Whatever had become of her friend Mr. Wilmuth, it seemed as if his absence had only a quieting effect upon Elizabeth ; for her face was bright, and a kind of smile touched and left her lips as she offered some word of excuse for delaying the two.

When they came to the hotel porch Mr. Ruley murmured a little at being so long left by himself.

" Miss Ruley met a friend "— unadvisedly began Graham, stopping short, however, with a late instinct of discretion.

" Of ours—from home ?" cut in the old man.

" No, no, papa !" said Elizabeth — a small

laugh actually rippling from her throat as she laid her hand on his white, rough hair—"a man I met since I've been away from Indiana."

" Why did you not bring him back to the hotel with you?" asked Mr. Ruley. " Your friends, my child, have — I may say, my warmest interest. I have often wished that the seclusion of your life were less extreme. You are but young."

" I'm but a lassie yet," smiled Elizabeth. And she took up lightly the song, pointing the words with pretty gestures, and leaning as she sang against the old man's shoulder. The fitful glaring of the curb-lamp, struggling with a defective carbon, discovered a soft dimple in her cheek, a clean-cut reft in her chin, the darkness and warmth in her eyes of the fruit of the wild blackthorn.

With this natural, girlish mood upon her, she was so unlike her usual cold and silent self that Wade had a visionary feeling in observing her. Against the yellow, lace-festooned windows of the lighted parlor she appeared quaint and fantastic, like a thing fashioned in a dream, and subject to irrational impulses which might cause her, on the sudden, to vanish and be nothing.

A smell of brine and honeysuckles came strong and sweet. When Elizabeth broke into a note of appreciation, saying, " I wish I had a great bunch of those fragrant yellow things," Wade rose.

" I will steal you some," he said. " They are hanging their honey temptingly near— on the next porch, in fact."

"You are, of course, merely jesting?" hesitated Mr. Ruley, already rising to go to his room for the night.

" Oh yes!" cried Wade. " I shall ask the owners."

When he came back presently with a lot of the dewy bells springing lustily from a mat of flaccid green leafage, he found Elizabeth alone. Graham had evidently attended her father up-stairs. She took the flowers eagerly, burying her face in their fresh amber.

" Are they stolen sweets?" she asked.

" Will it be a bond between us if they are?"

"Of friendship?—thieves do not have friends, but only evil associates."

"Oh, well," murmured Wade, losing himself a little, "friendship has its limitations! I'm not sure—" He paused with a slight embarrassment. Was he talking sentiment to the future wife of the Rev. Frederic Clinton Graham? He looked at Elizabeth. Over the bunch of honeysuckles, her face, faintly touched with smiles, with half-mocking provocation, with the insidious glamour of the moonlight, had a distracting, altogether unusual witchery. The young man was charmed, puzzled, disconcerted. Was this Elizabeth?

The noise of moving chairs and loitering feet broke through his muse. People were tramping back and forth in an interval of the ball-room music, and Wade felt the annoyance of a suddenly roused dreamer. He cast round upon the laughing crew a chastising eye.

"Do you mind the noises?" asked Elizabeth. "They are all so happy!"

"Maddeningly so," said Wade, with deep feeling.

"I forgive them," cried Elizabeth, softly. "I'm charitable to-night."

"Being yourself happier than usual?"

"Perhaps. I guess I've been quite contented all along, only I didn't show it, because I didn't know it! A person may not realize one mental condition till brought face to face with its opposite."

"Oh yes! averted peril teaches the sweetness of safety," said Wade. And then he chilled with a sharp sense of what this inadvertent remark might convey to her. But if she took it as an impertinence or a mere offshoot of self-evident philosophy, there was nothing in her manner to indicate either. Presently after she went away, and left him to the multitudinous loneliness of the jammed gallery.

As the days merged towards the end of August, Hildreth was packed to the very gates. The wiry yellow grasses along the neat walks were trampled into powder. The very sands, for all the effacing fingers of the tides, seemed never free of footprints, and by day and night the ocean promenade, the interior of the town, lake-sides, hotels, and the surf itself, were a press of holiday folk.

In these times Mr. Ruley seldom went

forth in his rolling-chair, except early of
a morning, when the beach was yet way-
free, and the sands unfrequented save for a
few barelegged men, who, with long wooden
rakes, cleaned up the sea-verge for the day.

Sometimes Wade pushed the chair. But
since the night when he gave Elizabeth the
honeysuckles he had in some measure avoided the old preacher's small circle. There had
been, on that occasion, a newness of impulse
in his spirit which made him feel the ad-
visability of keeping himself out of harm's
way, however sweet that way might seem.
Graham was the favored suitor. He, Wade,
having no chance for the rose, could at least
withhold his flesh from the thorn.

"So," said Grace Gayle, "you're out of
the running?"

"Ruled off," smiled Wade.

"Don't you make any mistakes," wisely
admonished Miss Gayle. "I've seen her look
at him, and I've seen her look at *you*."

"This is most surprising," indicated Wade,
with a feigned accent. "You will pardon
me, Gracie, if I scarcely credit your statement."

"Be sarcastic if you want to," said Gracie. "If you knew anything at all, you'd know that straws show which way the wind blows. When a woman regards a man with a kind of flat, frank sincerity, it's because her heart's altogether out of his reach. When she looks *around* him rather than *at* him, it's because—" Gracie lifted her shoulders suggestively.

"Grace," breathed Wade, gravely, "I am hurt to the quick to see you developing the germs of what painfully resembles thought. For Heaven's and your sex's sake, pause while there is yet time! Women who form the pernicious habit of thinking lose in time the magic key which unlocks the hearts of men."

Grace sniffed.

"Men's hearts are never locked," she said, sagaciously. "The heavier the padlock the smoother the hinges." She shook her crisp curls as she tripped away with her airy, mincing, soubrette tread.

Notwithstanding the inconsequent nature of this talk, it set Wade to thinking. Perhaps he had carried his principle of self-effacement too far. At all events, when he next saw Miss Ruley, he went up to her and stopped for a moment's conversation.

It chanced to be on the sands. Elizabeth was sitting by herself under the arch of a lace-hung sunshade, which cast shaking little shadows on her face, sprigging it with such delicate darknesses as lurk in the misty milk of moss-agate.

"You are going in, then?" she asked, smiling up rather uncertainly, and noticing his flannel attire. "Mr. Graham is already very far out. That is he, I think, taking that big breaker. What a stroke!"

Wade, focussing an indulgent eye, saw a figure away beyond the other bathers, rising to the lift of a great billow. The man swam with a splendid motion. Whether he dived, or floated, or circled his arms in that whirling stroke of his, he seemed in subtle sympathy with the sea, possessed of a kinship with it, and in an element altogether his own.

Wade expressed an appropriate sentiment of admiration.

Just then Gracie Gayle came gambolling along, a childish shape, kirtled to the knee

5

in bright blue, and turbaned in vivid scarlet. Among the loose-waisted figures on the sands she was like a humming-bird scintillating in a staid gathering of barn-yard fowls. Bailey was with her, having returned after a fortnight's absence.

The two paused beside Elizabeth, and Wade went on, confused by the singular way in which that small fair face, shadow-streaked and faintly smiling, lingered in his vision. He was still perplexed with a half-pleasant, half-pained consciousness of it as he plunged into the pushing surf and felt a dizzy world of water heave round him. The surge was strong to-day, and the splashing and screaming of the shore bathers sent him farther and still farther out. Gradually their cries lessened in his ear, and there was with him presently only the hollow thud of the waves and the rushing hiss of the cresting foam.

Once, as he rose to a sea-lift, it seemed to him that he heard a sound that was not the boom of the breakers nor the song of the slipping froth. It came again, whatever it was, and as he gave ear he took in a human

" ' MR GRAHAM IS ALREADY FAR OUT ' "

intonation, sharp and agonized. It was a cry for help.

Wade shook the brine from his hair, freeing his gaze for an outlook. In the glassy mound of water to his right a face, lean and white with alarm, gleamed and faded. That the sinking man was Graham came instantly to Wade's mind—Graham, a victim to some one of the mischances which the sea reserves for those who adventure too confidently with her.

Wade struck out instantly for the spot where Graham's appalled features had briefly glimpsed. Shoreward he could note an increasing agitation among the multitudes. Evidently the people had noticed the peril of the remote swimmer whose exploits had so lately won admiring comment. The beach-guard no doubt was buckling to his belt the life-rope coiled always on the sands for such emergencies. Cries of men and women rang stifled over the water—exclamations of fear and advice and excitement, mingled in a long continuous wail.

Graham's head rose in sight, a mere speck upon the dense green of the bulging water.

Wade, fetching nearer in wide strokes, suddenly felt himself twisted violently out of his course, and whirled round in a futile effort with some mysterious current. He was almost near enough to lay hold of Graham when this new sensation explained lucidly the cause of Graham's danger. They were both in the claws of an undertow, which, as Wade realized its touch, appeared as if wrenching him straight out to the purring distance of the farther sea.

Even in the first consternation of this discovery he felt himself thrust hard against a leaden body, and in the same instant Graham's hands snatched at him in a desperate reach for life.

" For God's sake don't hold me like this!" Wade expostulated. " Let go. Trust me to do what I can. You're strangling me, man!"

But Graham was past sanity. He only clutched with the more frenzy at the thing which seemed to keep him from the ravenous mouth of the snarling waters.

Wade, in a kind of composed despair, sent a look towards the beach. They were putting out a boat, a tiny shell which frisked in the surf, and seemed motionless in the double action of the waves. Men laid hard at the oars. The little craft took the first big wave as a horse takes a hurdle. It dropped from the glassy height, and Wade saw it sink into a breach of the sea. Then, flashing with crystal, it bore up again and outward.

The figures running and gesticulating on the beach had a marvellous distinctness to Wade's submerging eyes. He noticed the blue sky, flawed with scratches of white, the zigzag roof-lines of the great town, the twisting flags and meshes of dark wire. Everything oppressed him with a sort of deadly clearness, as if a metal stamp should press in melting wax.

He was momently sinking, drawn ever outward by the undercurrent, and downward by the weighty burden throttling him in its senseless grasp. He looked once more through a blinding veil of foam, and saw the boat dipping far to the left. A phantasm of life flickered before him. Unsuspected trivialities shook out of their cells, and amazed him with the pygmy thrift of memory. Then came a sense of confusion, as if the spiritual and corporal lost each its boundary and ranged wild, and Wade felt the sea in his eyes, stroking them down as gently as ever any watcher by the dying.

GRACE GAYLE had flung herself in the hot sand near Elizabeth.

"What made Mr. Wade go away the minute I came?" she asked. "Had you been saying something unkind to him, or did I simply queer a friendly talk by dropping down on you?"

She lay at length, listening to Elizabeth's word of reply.

"Well," said Bailey, presently, "I guess I'll travel, unless you're going in before long?"

Grace lifted herself on an elbow and commanded him to wait a minute. She was gazing thoughtfully out upon the waste of water, and turning a little hollow in the sand with one slim foot.

"I sha'n't stay in long to-day," she said. "It looks pretty heavy, that surf. How hard that man away out there is swimming! It must be a bet." She stared with keener interest, and as the others followed her gaze she rose upon her knees for a better range.

A sudden commotion had arisen in the throng under the pavilion. A man's voice shouted excitedly, and a woman's scream shrilled out. ,

"An accident," decided Bailey. "Some one's got beyond his depth." He scrutinized the distance, and the remote figure swimming vigorously across the reach of sea. Elizabeth had risen also, and the three stood staring out.

"He won't reach him!" cried a young fellow hard by; "though he's a fine stroke—Wade is."

"Wade!" cried Gracie, wheeling—"Wade! Is that—"

"Selby Wade, the newspaper—why, he stops at your hotel, Miss Gayle. The fellow that's sinking stops there too. I don't know his name. Big man—with a shaved face. I've noticed him rolling some old man in a chair."

Elizabeth Ruley had uttered a little gasping kind of cry. She swayed forward, and without seeming to see Bailey, caught at his

arm to stay herself. Bailey himself was unaware of everything except that far-off struggle, and the action of the beach-guards.

"They've got the boat out!" he cried, as
the pointed thing spun back and forth in the
counter-currents like a red shuttle. Grace
had hidden her face against one of the heavy
posts supporting the pavilion.

"O Blessed Mary!" she kept muttering
with dry lips. "O Holy Mother, save him
—save them, I mean! Oh, be merciful! O
Lord, help him! help him! 'I make promise
of amendment'—oh, what's the rest of it?—
'I make promise of amendment'—ah, yes!—
'amendment, moved to great love and tender
pity at sight of Thy five precious wounds.'"

Her voice was lost in the outcries about
her. Men called loudly to each other and
to the oarsmen. Women sobbed and covered
their eyes.

"He's got hold of him!" rang out, as the
struggling swimmer seemed to snatch at the
shoulder of the drowning man. Then an appalled murmur arose.

"It's an underpull!"

"They're going out!"

" The boat ! The boat ! She won't make it."

" Faster, you fellows !—They're sinking !"

The indefinite atom of humanity warring out there with the piled-up power of the ocean seemed indeed to give over the struggle. An oily sweep of sea poured round the spot where the men's heads had fitfully lifted. There was an instant's silent waiting for the reappearance of those dark flecks in the farther sea. Then a cry rang wildly up— " Lost ! Lost !"

In this moment the hot grasp on Bailey's bare arm relaxed so suddenly as to recall him to a sense of the woman beside him. She was wheeling dizzily, with the motion of one about to fall, but still struggling with a waning consciousness. Her eyes were half shut ; but the wonted fixity of her features was broken into an expression of such impassioned horror that, as Bailey, thrusting out a hand to steady the circling figure, observed the strange difference of her anguish-stricken face, his own eyes started wide.

" Ah !" he said, " where have your wits been, Bailey ? You were not mistaken."

VII

IF there was anything at all coherent in Wade's mind, as he felt the sea pulling over him, it was a fierce sort of resentment that the little tossing boat should be so futilely near. A fraction of a moment meant life to him now—the merest fraction of a moment. And all the while the boat hovered round him like a hawk, and the weight on his shoulders dragged more and more inertly. That weight! —but for that weight of clinging, half-conscious manhood— A sudden fierce impulse, not in the least humane, but born of the desperation of stifling breath, darted through Wade's gasping senses. He gathered himself and wrenched free one arm, and with it struck blindly out and smote Graham between the shut eyes.

Instantly the man's grasp loosened. But with the vivifying sense of buoyancy which this relaxation gave to Wade rose an instinct

of humanity only a degree less cogent than
had been the feeling which prompted the
blow. He laid lightly hold of the other's
shoulder, and held him somehow or other
afloat for the next second, till the hover-
ing little craft fetched near enough for
aid.

Even then it was hard enough to get Graham aboard. And after this was accom-
plished it seemed as if, after all, help had
come too late; for the young preacher lay
like a log in the boat, only gasping once or
twice as they turned him. Before they made
the shore, however, he began to fetch gur-
gling breaths, and Wade, observing him, decided that all would presently be well with
Miss Ruley's lover.

For the first time his mind recurred keenly
to Elizabeth. Sitting on the beach she had,
of course, seen the whole matter of Graham's
misadventure, and was, no doubt, still unaware that the rescuers had been in time to
save him. Wade experienced a strong sentiment of gratitude at the sickening heave of
Graham's broad chest. The young man was
going to be deadly ill, without doubt, but at

least he, Wade, would not have to break to Elizabeth the news of her lover's death.

When the boat nosed the sands and people pressed about it with reaching hands and hot words of enthusiastic congratulation, Wade lapsed into rather a surly state, put about by the free expressions of approval lavished on what the beach multitudes elected to term his heroic deed. Waiving all this with disgusted embarrassment, the young man was nevertheless obliged to smile at the tearful incoherence with which Gracie Gayle rushed upon him and clasped his hands.

" And Graham?" she panted, as a sort of after-thought; " is he alive?"

" I should say so! He'll be all right presently. Does Miss Ruley know "— He paused, having just caught sight of her in a momentary breach of the crowd, leaning upon Bailey's arm and looking whiter than the foam at her feet. He hurried towards her.

" He's all right," he burst out, reassuringly —" Graham. He's a little sickish just now, but "— Again he broke off. Elizabeth Ruley, lifting her face in a sudden, moved kind of way, looked him mutely in the eyes.

He had seen it variously sad, musing, anxious, and apprehensive—that still, chill glance beneath her straight brows; but he had never dreamed that it or any other gaze could quicken his very soul with such a sense as burned there now, a sense making his own eyes lift in a spasm of feeling which shut his lips hard upon a sharp, short, rapturous breath.

A number of the hotel people closed about her. Without a word Wade gave way to them. There was no need to say anything whatever. The profound consciousness which had leaped upon him in that single instant was not a thing to break easily at the lips.

With an illusory sense upon him, he went up to the bath-houses, and, still feeling like one meshed in the glittering woof of a delicious dream, on to the Dorsheimer Arms. How had he been able, during these past weeks, to delude himself into believing he should suffer little in resigning this woman to a life in which he had no part? Had it been he, indeed, who had calmly figured her as shining with serene sweetness in the home and parish of the Rev. Frederic Clinton Graham? Wade laughed out in scorn of the no-

tion. He set his lips and narrowed his eyes
even to think of such a thing.

" Why," he murmured, amazedly, " I love
her more than life itself. I would die for her."
These assurances burst out with strength, if
lacking absolute originality of phrase. In a
moment he himself laughed to remember that
he had heard other men make such statements,
and had been faintly amused at the prodigal-
ity of love's vows and the curious sameness
of its figures of speech.

Sitting on the edge of his bed, he covered
his eyes and drifted into a beatific world, all
a riot of blue skies and scattered roses and
clasping cupids and pastoral pipes. Elizabeth glided through the ferny greenness—
Elizabeth, in floating white, with a ribbon
of girlish blue in the shadowy depths of her
hair — Elizabeth, with handfuls of honeysuckles, no longer still and loath, but glad and
smiling, warm and heartening as the flowers
she bore. And then presently these Arca-
dian alleys lapsed to ways not less sweet,
though more familiar. A walled-up city street
stretched out before him, narrow and mo-
notonous, with its tall dwellings and meagre

ribbon of sky. Was this one of the apartments he had so hated—this reach of rooms, tunnelled with a long dark hall, with sunshine only in snatches, and with strange cubby-holes crouching about shafts which mouthed up a dim, infernal light? It seemed to have inconsequent features in common with his old detestation; but it could not be the same, for this range of rooms radiated delight—being, indeed, pervaded with a presence which, to Wade's mind, would have shed a gentle home-rapture upon a section of the Catacombs.

He could hear the ripple of Elizabeth's gown, the soft fall of her foot as she moved through those pictured spaces. Elizabeth!—he had never known before that it was his favorite name. He repeated it to himself till it lost meaning and startled him with its strangeness. He wished to see her at once, yet dreaded to see her, as inevitably he must, among others.

At this juncture there was a rap at his door, and when he opened it he saw Mr. Ruley standing in the hall.

"Frederic wants to see you," said the old man, tremulous with emotion. "He is ad-

vised by the doctor to lie by for the day, being
er—somewhat—"

"Salt-water has that effect generally. He'll
brace up after a bit."

"I trust so! I trust so! snatched thus by
the unspeakable goodness of God from the
fate of them that go down in ships. Ah, my
young friend, blessed indeed are those that
are ordained to be instruments of His grace.
I have come to fetch you to the bedside of
this dear soul that he may, in such sort as he
is directed, make acknowledgment to you
for your timely aid." He fondly laid hold
of Wade's arm.

"He'll feel more like falling on my neck
when his stomach settles!" laughed Wade.
"I'll wait till then." But Mr. Ruley drew
him down the corridor with that singularly
forceful strength which occasionally showed
itself in his lank, leaning form.

Graham turned a qualmish face upon them.

"I can't say a word," he declared. "I've
a lot of pretty speeches laid up for emergencies, but none for one like this. I never
foresaw having my life saved. I guess you
know how I feel!"

6

"Yes. I saw you were swallowing too much brine," said Wade. He added, "Sorry I had to punch your head!" The two men smiled over their clasped hands.

"Ah!" cried Mr. Ruley, gazing with distended rheumy eyes upon this fraternal picture, "Frederic was saved to great works, being specially favored in his holy calling, and specially gifted with rare persuasive qualities."

"Oh!" murmured Graham, deprecatingly.

"I speak the fact," protested the other. "I myself have been very zealous for the Lord of Hosts. I cried aloud, and showed my people their transgressions. I depicted to them hell enlarging herself and opening her mouth without measure. Sabbath after Sabbath I told them that their glory, their pomp, and their multitude should descend therein. But they were puffed up and given to their idols. They would not hear. They had no pleasure in the words of the servant of the Most High."

Wade and Graham exchanged a glance which expressed no surprise that Mr. Ruley's congregation had failed to accept his views with joyous alacrity.

"I strove mightily with a perverse and stiff-necked generation. I told them of their loathsome iniquity, of their guile, their vanity, their shame, their utterly lost condition. They heard me," cried Mr. Ruley, in a bitterly sonorous voice, "with the apathy of them that are dead according to the law. Yet I saw those stubborn hearts softened. Another than I spoke to them, and, behold, the flint was melted. To Him be the honor who hast ordained this miracle of victorious young priesthood—Frederic, my son in the faith!" His quavering accents broke and the fierceness left his beaked face.

Graham looked at Wade and shrugged his shoulders.

"I reap where you sowed," he said, considerately. A flash leaped to the old man's deep eyes.

"You speak with the voice of the comforter," he sighed, shaking his rough white hair, but visibly pleased.

During the entire day Wade saw nothing of Elizabeth. At supper, however, his heart gave an unaccustomed twitch as he observed her dark head in a distant end of the dining-

room. He hung about the office till she came
out, carrying her father's shawl, and prepared
to fix him comfortably on the porch.

Her eyes avoided Wade, but as she passed
him a little breath of pink fluctuated in her
cheek, whereat the young man took exceeding heart, being happily unaware that his
tender observance of Miss Ruley was winning
amused smiles from the people about.

Gracie Gayle brushed up to him.

" It's all right, then ? Will papa live with
you? poor old dear! He's a back number,
but he means well. Only this wicked world's
no place for men like him. Folks never
thank you for telling them they've got soot
on their noses. They'd rather be jollied
up a little, and made to think their faces
are pretty clean. Hum ?—the Rev. Graham,
now. I'm willing to put up my European
successes that he'll be right in it for luck!
He'll have a big city pulpit and his sermons
printed in the newspapers. You mark my
words. He's up to date ; and I'm proud of
you, Wade—awful proud of you for beating
his time, for I saw the way you and Elizabeth acted just now when she passed, and I

was right on. I knew it was all right." She
waved her hand back at him as she fluttered
up-stairs, all a maze of rosy muslin, with a
tinkling of silver bangles on her wrists.

Wade resolutely approached his friends in
the porch corner.

"Don't let me interfere with your usual
walk," said Mr. Ruley. "Go while it is yet
light, Elizabeth—you and our good friend.
I shall presently seek Frederic's side. He
wishes to consult me upon a question which
my acquaintance with the early fathers justi-
fies me in discussing." Blessing him pro-
foundly, Wade moved his chair back and
looked questioningly at Elizabeth.

She rose with an air of reluctance, and they
went down the steps together and into the
thronged street, which queerly enough seemed
to Wade a cosmic wilderness whose sweet
solitude was peopled only by himself and the
girl at his side.

As he talked of common things he took
her silence comfortably to heart. No doubt
she felt this singular atmosphere, which had
so suddenly ensphered them in a new world.
That was it. She was moved by the strange-

ness of it all, and felt, as indeed he himself felt, a little stupefied, a little dazed by the greatness of the difference. So Wade decided as they came to the ocean side.

Dim, phantom sails reached into the fading sky. One schooner lay at anchor off the bar. A rich brownish chrome streaked its flat foresail, and upon the mingling tones of sky and sea its rigging trailed a delicate filigree of black. Through the zigzag spaces of a distant pavilion shone, as through a dark trellis, the shattered amber of the west. Against it one white arc-lamp hung like a jewel. Other lights spun out from the half-gloom of the town. The crowd on the walk thickened. It grew, with every instant, more and still more noisy. Sound and movement ingulfed the comparative quietude, and there was nothing presently to tell of its briefly tranquil charm except the motionless vessel lying out there at sea and visibly melting into the dark bosom of the night. A low tide whined on the sands. Off to the left the little lake, thrusting out in the sunset glow from its wooded belt, looked like a dagger of gold in a dark girdle.

"Let us walk round that way," suggested
Wade. They turned towards the sliver of
burnished water, the color of which, as they
neared it, waned to a mere dull russet. About
the rim were tall lamps, which plunged blunt,
leaden shafts of light into the still depths.
A little bridge rose over the expanse, and as
they mounted its soft curve a boat shot below them and the voices of the rowers rang
upward.

Then a soft stillness settled down. A gray
density of shadow crept stealthily from a
tiny wooded island just beyond the bridge,
and some bird in the dark leafage chirped a
long, lonely note.

Elizabeth, leaning on the slight rail, herself
half folded in shadow, stood watching the
lucid trail of the vanishing boat. Wade,
filled with the simple happiness of her presence, set his elbow on the balustrade and let
the sweetness of the moment encompass him.
All the fulness of complete knowledge might
never be so exquisite a thing as this " prodi-
gal inward joy," as yet unaverred except by
the forces of life which speak without lan-
guage.

And as he leaned there, rapt in the enchantment which silence and assurance com-
bined to work upon him, another skiff
flashed into sight, daubing the water with
thin vermilion from the red light it bore. A
girl's voice, bold and clear, lilted up the bars
of a song made popular by some concert-hall
favorite—a song none too reticent of illusion,
with a reckless swing of rhythm and a de-
mure suggestiveness of phrase.

Darting shafts of scarlet about it, the boat
struck under the bridge. In emerging it disclosed a boyish young fellow at the oars, and
opposite him, in a cloud of airy pink, the
small singer. Gracie's gold slippers cast off
a gay gleam, as if she were shod with sunshine. Her bangles flashed and clashed as
she idly shredded up the bunch of roses in
her lap and flung the petals in her companion's face. He, bending his blonde head,
laughed at the soft pelting. Then, quickly
enough, he drew both oars into one hand,
and, reaching forward, caught the girl's teasing fingers.

She paused in her song and laughed. Em-
boldened, he lifted the little hand. His lips

"THEN A SOFT STILLNESS SETTLED DOWN"

had not touched it, however, when she
snatched it away.

"Mind your oars," she advised him, taking
up the rollicking measure again and casting
a wind of pink flowers over the skiff-side.

Wade straightened himself with a consciousness of strong distaste. His conviction
of Gracie's ability to take care of herself
was, if anything, deepened by this episode.
But he had a moral qualm at the girl's suf-
ficiency, because it bore so emphatic a hint
of much experience. From the swift impres-
sion of her mirthful mockery, her acute
glance, her cheek, altogether unabashed at
man's approving, and her whole piquant,
theatric personality, Wade's vision returned
to the figure beside him, poised with a little
air of meditation and with gentle gaze bent
on the shaken redness of the lake.

"Elizabeth!" he said, suddenly put to
speech, "oh, what a rapture it is just to
stand here with you! Dearest love, tell me
that I don't misunderstand your silence! I
couldn't care like this, could I, for a woman
who did not love me a little?" Something
like a shivering coldness went over him. She

had distinctly shrunk away from him, and
even in the shadows it seemed as if her face
assumed an austere fixity.

"I beg of you," she stammered, "do not
—do not—"

"But, Elizabeth!" besought Wade, shaken
with misgivings, "listen!—oh, be generous
with me! no one will ever love you as I do.
It's my life you have in your hands." He
was beyond that half-humorous criticism
which he commonly brought to bear on himself no less than on others. If what he said
had been often said in precisely the tone in
which he now poured it hotly forth, he did
not think or care. "I know how unworthy
I am, dearest. But you can make me anything you will — anything. Oh, Elizabeth!
just now when I saw that poor little girl
in her stagey finery, with her safe reckless-
ness and pertness and sharp wisdom, I thanked
God that my fate was, in loving you, my pure
little saint, to love upward to the highest
reach of my ideals. Oh, you can't know what
it is to me, that sweet cloistral air of yours,
that gentle reserve! You have been shut
away from the world and its knowledges, and

I am more glad than I can say, my love, my wife—"

"I have asked you not to say any more," Elizabeth broke in, speaking with haste, almost with sharpness. •

" But—"

"No more. It is impossible, impossible!" As she said this, however, her voice broke and her head fell on her breast.

"Oh," she murmured, " *how* impossible I pray you may never know! For I care—yes, I want you to know that I care—greatly for your—regard and—respect."

VIII

In dwelling upon Elizabeth's words and manner, Wade felt like one in the thick of a cloud, which, without assuming shape itself, confuses and thwarts the view. Through it, however, like a storm-blurred star, the radiance of her own confession of regard shone bright.

He had besought some explanation of her meaning, but she had said only that if he cared for her at all he would show it best by asking nothing ; that if he was generous he would take her attitude as final and necessary. And while he was yet asking her to show a little confidence in him, she had passed hurriedly up the wide steps of the hotel and crossed the office and turned the bend of the stairs. Since which time he had seen her no more, though a day had dragged by.

He wandered round the place, tormented by his own restlessness as well as by the sounds and sights which the outer world forced on his irritated sensibilities. It was as if these objective annoyances were grotesquely magnified by the lens of pain through which he saw them. Everything was an offence, and affected him as the tiniest pressure affects a bruise.

Graham, striding down the long dining-room, was a maddening sight in his breezy light-heartedness. The fair locks of a young widow at his own table, whose grief expressed itself in a mixture of heavy crape and numerous diamonds, impressed him with a hideous falsity of hue. A child wailed out, and was borne away by some one who rose and pushed a chair about on the polished floor. In a spasm of revolt Wade thrust back from the table and left it all behind—that clamorous apartment filled with a long perspective of ceaselessly gleaming knives and forks. Yet even in these hours of utter dissatisfaction it was almost amusing to him to reflect that this babel of noise and movement represented to so many people an ideal state of enjoyment.

"Elizabeth," said Mr. Ruley, after supper,

" will not join us this evening. She is suffering with what seems to be a slight headache. Truly affliction is the ordinary feature of mortal destiny."

After a time Graham and Wade strolled off together, taking their way through some interior streets of the town, upon the comparative darkness of which the lights of cottages broke in a peaceful, domestic fashion wholly different from the way of the beach precincts, all glaring with electricity.

Through open doors they caught sight of family gatherings, of children playing, of young folk talking, of an old woman bending soberly over a thick book. Graham, looking up at the stars, gave a sigh.

" They're the things that really count, after all," he asserted. " If a man misses it—love, you know, and home ties—nothing else ever perfectly makes it up to him. We are told with high-handed scorn that love isn't much of a power, anyway; that it means little in comparison with life's other forces. But I believe it's a pretty big thing, myself. There's a time in a fellow's career when it counts for a devilish deal. It's a power."

"GRAHAM WAS A MADDENING SIGHT IN HIS BREEZY
LIGHT-HEARTEDNESS"

Wade agreed with this view, and Graham pushed on : " I've an idea that there's only one pair of hands in the world that can kindle the flame on a man's hearth. And if he makes a mistake and gets the wrong pair, he'll have a sickly warmth in his inglenook."

Wade lifted his brows, surmising what the specialized nature of this figure portended.

" Yes," pursued Graham, " a man, in my mind, does well to subordinate other things to love. He'd better marry the woman who pleases him even if he has to sacrifice something in the way of ambition and that kind of thing."

" If she will have him," added Wade.

" No trouble about that. Women marry the men who ask them." He laughed, and laid a confidential hand on Wade's arm.

"Of course you've seen what's in the wind? I'm pretty hard hit. That little witch has turned my head with her shy, stately ways. And a clergyman ought to marry. He owes it to his people. Elizabeth is as retiring as the traditional wood-violet, but in a different atmosphere—for I don't propose to stay forever in Indiana—I think she'll expand to the social necessities of her position as my wife. I admired her from the first. There's something unaccountable about her that catches a fellow's imagination. But I went slow. It's a big decision for a man. And it wasn't an advantageous alliance for me—looking at it in cold blood. But the more I see of her the harder I'm nailed. I've made up my mind to settle everything before I leave here —I've got to go soon now. My time's up."

He began to whistle "Annie Laurie" between his teeth. They had returned to the threshold of the Dorsheimer Arms, and, seeing Grace Gayle sitting by herself in the porchway, Wade stopped for a moment.

"I've been looking for you," she said. "Something's out of gear. Your face gives it away. And when I rapped at Elizabeth's door just now to see how her headache was, I noticed that her eyes were swelled up. She's been crying. Yes, crying," she repeated impressively, as Wade started. "It broke me all up to see how bad she looked. I know something's up. You'd better let me in on the ground-floor, Wade. Neither you nor her has any better friend than me. I'd do a good deal for you."

"Thanks, Titania," muttered Wade, gloomily. "Your barley - sugar wand can't do anything for me just now." He paused with a weary air and added: "That poor young fellow over there at the cooler—hadn't you better look after him a little? He seems desperate—he's drinking altogether too much iced water. Isn't he the chap who was rowing you last night?—his joy was brief."

"I'm not worrying about him," snapped Gracie, pettishly. "Indifference is good for a man."

> "'They fish with all nets
> In the school of coquettes,'"

Wade quoted. "The wing of recompense will darken your unfeeling brow some day, my lady. You will then understand"— He paused, smiling, for Grace had flounced angrily away.

Presently after this, Bailey, searching round the thronged piazza for her, came upon her in an isolated corner.

"By yourself?" asked Bailey, pleasantly

7

surprised at the absence of Grace's usual court. "I'm in luck. I wanted a word with you. I'm going up to town to-morrow. And I thought I'd get your final—"

"Oh, bother!" exclaimed Grace. "I'm in no mood for talking business. But I may as well tell you, once for all, that I've about decided to stay with Vaughn. He did the square thing by me last season. He'll feature me, and all that. I'd of liked the best kind to join you," explained the girl more kindly. "I know you're a hustler; but mom don't like to travel, and I'm fond of the city. You'll get some one quite as good as I am."

"There's Daisy Higby," reflected Bailey. "She's got a new dance that they say will catch on immensely." Grace started.

"She's good style," she admitted, generously; "not very original, but rather graceful, and all that."

"She hasn't your go; but she's popular. I'd set my heart on having you, Gracie; but if I can't make it I'll have to do the next best. We're old friends. I remember you when you were a slip of a thing in the chorus of—"

"Don't remind me of it!" gasped Gracie.

" Miserable little thing I was! The folks
that saw me dancing in pink tulle didn't
dream what a ragged frock I changed it for
after the curtain. I was saving every cent
to pay for dancing-lessons. I might have
been struggling to this day but for Wade's
write-up. I'll never forget what I owe him—
though he treats me with scorn!" she added, in a burst of resentment.

" Scorn! why—"

" Oh, well, maybe not just scorn; but
when I try to help him—he's in a kind of a
hole at present—he simply laughs at me, and
politely advises me to mind my own affairs.
It's rough; that's what."

" Is Wade in a hole? He seemed in high
feather yesterday afternoon."

" I can't explain," said Miss Gayle, with
dignity. " He wouldn't like to have his affairs discussed. But it's a love—"

" Ah !"

" A love-affair," frowned Gracie. " You've
noticed him and Miss Ruley, I suppose? I
thought everything was settled; but something's gone wrong. I'd give a good deal to
find out just what."

Bailey sat on the porch-rail staring at his cigarette.

"Jove!" he said. "I guess I could give you the cue to the situation. I guess it's Miss Ruley that's made the difficulty. She's got a—well, a kind of a reason that might make her act queer in a case like this. I don't say it's a good reason, but it's the sort of thing that would make matters a little hard if she cared for a man and had to explain."

Grace's eyes flashed in the darkness of the side-porch.

"Bailey!" she cried, "how glad I am I spoke of this business! Go on—go on and tell me!"

But Bailey suddenly stiffened.

"I'd like to," he signified, "but it wouldn't be straight. What I didn't drop to myself a fellow I've met since I was in the city this last trip told me in dead confidence—man named Wilmuth. Honest, Gracie, I can't give it away. Don't ask me. I can't do it."

"Look here!" cried Gracie. "I'm dying to know what you're onto. Tell me, Bailey! I'll do anything—I'm not sure, after all, but

I'll sign with you. Yes, Bailey ; you tell me. I'm going to sign with you !"

The next instant she saw her mistake. Bailey's boyish eyes hardened.

" I wish to God you hadn't said that," he declared. " You must have a dead-low opinion of me. I don't make any bluff about honor and that rot. I'm no man in a story-book to split hairs and beat his conscience into a froth ; but you better believe I'm not going to sell my soul for your signature."

He cast his cigarette away with an indignant motion. His head was up, his jaws set. He looked down upon the girl in the chair with a glance of steady contempt.

Grace watched him with surprise. Was this Bailey—the mild, conciliating Bailey— always politic, always bent with gentle, and often unscrupulous, determination on his own ends—this man with the squared chin and scathing eyes ?

Something like admiration crept into Gracie's shrewd gaze—something stirred in her heart.

" Bailey," she said, impulsively, " I admire you more this minute than I ever did or ever expected to. You've always seemed to me just a manager. You strike me now as a *man.* I'm glad I tempted you—or tried to tempt you—if only to find out what *kind* of a man you really are. Here's my hand on it, Bailey!"

Bailey's cast-iron mood dropped off. He breathed a little uncertainly as he took her warmly proffered fingers. He was even more disturbed as he saw on Gracie's face, upheld in the half-gloom, an expression of honest and simple sincerity.

"Gracie," he said, "I didn't think you'd ever make a fool of *me!* I thought I was proof against your little tricks. But, by Jove! when you look like that — like a dear little kind-hearted woman instead of a—"

"Go on."

"You know what I mean!—don't tell me to go on unless you want to hear—that—that—"

"Well?"

"Oh, the devil!—I might know you don't care a rap! Good-bye, Gracie." He turned angrily on his heel, put about by the light mockery of Grace's tone. But this accent had altogether vanished when she lifted her voice and said, very softly, " Bailey !"

He turned. She was leaning forward, smiling rather gravely.

" Grace," he said, still standing away and speaking brusquely, " be plain. You're not fooling with a boy. It's dead serious with me. Are you in earnest ?"

" If I should be—"

He flung himself beside her.

" If you care for me, Gracie, if you care—"

She laughed softly.

" If I didn't," she said, presently, " you can bet your arm wouldn't be where it is now !"·

IX

On the next morning Wade had a passing glimpse of Elizabeth, as he stood in the office unfolding the heavy sheets of the Sunday paper.

"Ah," said a deep utterance behind him, "it grieves me, my friend, to see this! It is a reprobate nation that pollutes His day with such like. They are ill-fitted for the Word who first fill themselves with the contents of a news-sheet." Wade smiled a little under the long denunciative finger pointing at the journal in his hands. He was less aware of it than of the figure coming along behind Mr. Ruley's tall form.

The two were going to church apparently, for Elizabeth carried a little black book, from which a narrow purple ribbon hung. There was a kind of sorrowful composure in her soft features.

"'Cold, cold, my girl!'" murmured Wade

to himself, in a pained acceptance of her attitude, as she passed by, giving him a sense
of something chill and sweet and unearthly
as a breath from a flower-set altar. Upon
that vision of her he was obliged to nourish
his thoughts all day, for, after the morning
service, she went up-stairs and reappeared no
more. On the edge of dark he saw Graham
and Mr. Ruley setting forth as if to some
meeting which a distant church-bell was an-
nouncing.

At the head of the steps they paused, being accosted by Miss Gayle, who floated from
her mother's side and joined them.

"Where is Miss Ruley?" she asked. "I
want to see her about something special."
The old preacher surveyed, with a certain
pious tolerance, the small white-clad shape at
his elbow.

"She is in her room," he said, "and feeling less like herself than I could wish. I
think she would scarcely desire to be disturbed
just now, since she was—I may say—unable
to accompany us to divine service."

"She'll be down after a while," Graham
assured Gracie, with a glance appreciative of

the rose-dashed lips and curled black hair of
the small person beyond him. "I think she
said, sir, that she would join us on the porch
upon our return?"

"I believe so," owned the old man. "Come,
Frederic. Let us not offend the Most High,
as so many are wont, by appearing late in
His house."

Wade, not overhearing this brief talk, observed the emptying piazza with growing
gloom. A "sacred concert" was forward in
one of the big beach-stands, and people were
moving down the street in waxing multitudes.
Joining these throngs, Wade, with his hat sulk-
ing over his eyes, found himself at first indif-
ferent to the extraordinary crush of the promenade. In both directions a sweeping host
pushed, and as he took in, with perhaps a certain acerbity of criticism, the mass of people,
it seemed to Wade that only by the seldom-
est occasion any individual had the slightest
distinction of feature, bearing, or apparel.

Muslins and laces and flowers and per-
fumes and pink cheeks and dimples and curls
mixed in a definite aggregation of commonplace youthful prettiness. Matronly silks

touched the scene with spots of purple and black. Scarcely any men beyond middle age were to be seen, and at this hour no children whatever. A gratifying lack of pretension marked the crowd. Only now and then a rich toilet walked sublime among the home-wrought frocks of the women-folk, a splendor commonly fitting the lavish contours of some middle-aged lady, whose heavily prosperous air seemed a little new to her.

No one appeared to care much for the chalky reach of sea dashing its lime-white powder on the sands. The sky, all dappled with bronze, hung low and bright. A soft wind whirred in from the ocean, and as it darkened beyond twilight a distant yacht disclosed itself as a mere blur of orange in the gathering shadows.

Feeling out of harmony with the great good cheer of the crowd, Wade started back to the hotel. The town had a singular aspect of loneliness, having poured its thousands out upon the verge of the sea. Streets and porches looked deserted. Electric lights burned with a waste luxuriance over the empty spaces, like candles set by the dead. The very stars glimmered far and pale, and suddenly, as Wade looked up, one of them shot out of space, burning a long scar in the dark face of the night.

That fading cleft of saffron gave the young man an odd feeling of human littleness and individual desolation, and this was not dissipated by the absolutely forsaken aspect of the Dorsheimer Arms. The piazza was a long vista of empty chairs. The very office had only one occupant — a bell - boy sitting asleep on the bench below the signal-board.

An enchantment of silence hung upon everything. But as Wade's foot rang loud on the threshold, there vibrated through the strange stillness of the place a sound which drew him motionless. The sound of a voice, it was, bitter and sharp, and echoing from the bare expanse of the reading-room.

"Never," it swept out strong and stern — "never shall I overlook this abomination you have worked. According to your treachery another than I shall deal with you, yea, according to the measure of your sin. I cannot wonder that you weep. It would be past all hardihood if you were not something confounded with your shame. Oh, that you had died in the hour that gave you birth! That I had rendered you back to God, pure in your infancy, than that you had lived to turn and pollute my name now when my hands are waxed feeble! Yea, God! Thou hast scourged me with rods, Thou hast poured me out like water, Thou hast smitten me in the work of my hands, and I have been silent. Now I am laid waste utterly. I am in the dust. I am uprooted and dishonored!"

Wade had stepped forward. The single gas-jet in the reading-room flickered low, and in the centre of the dimly-lighted room the old Indiana preacher stood tall and terrible, with an outstretched, anathematizing hand. Three others were in the apartment — Graham, just beyond the old man, touched an averted face with a troubled finger; against the post of the ball-room door Grace Gayle leaned, pale, with scared eyes and breathless lips; and immediately before her father, shrinking, cowering under his harsh outpour of words, Elizabeth Ruley stood covering her white face with two trembling hands.

" Don't—oh, don't—condemn me so utterly !" she moaned. " I don't try to—to excuse myself. I have sinned, father—yes, yes! But we had nothing, nothing to live on ! I couldn't see you take the—the miserable pension the church that turned you off would have flung to you in charity ! Father, no ! Believe me— oh, believe me !—it wasn't for myself that I wronged you — that I sold myself—that I practised this shameful deceit ! It was for you—for—"

" Do not dare," broke in the old man, with a fearful gleam in his wrathful face, " to make me the apology of your iniquity. Better I had starved than that this should have come upon me. Have I loved life so as to purchase it at such a price ? No ! Upon your own head be the reward of your evil ! for I stand henceforth aside from your deceits. You are no issue of mine, who am left desolate, betrayed even by my own loins." He swung on his heel, and brushed off, with an imperious gesture, the hands of the woman who had fallen down before him and would have clasped his knees.

Graham, with a motion of helpless pain, wheeled past Grace Gayle and into the dark-

ness of the dance-hall. Grace hung against
the door, mute and motionless, as the old man
strode towards the office. In its hard impla-
cability his face looked like a mask of iron.
His gaze was fierce and fixed, and a vigor beyond the mere vigor of young blood stirred
in his long gait and swinging arms. And
where he had left her Elizabeth crouched,
with forlorn face bent upon him, and with
one miserably shaking hand even yet reaching after him in piteous appeal.

Viewing this concentrated presentment of
human passion, altogether unintelligible to
him except in its effects, Wade's breath came
quick. A tumult of generous impulse surged
in him, and his heart lifted as if a great flood
bore it up. He jostled the old man's obdu-
rate form as he passed it in his haste.

"Elizabeth," he said, lifting her, and heed-
less of the girl in the doorway who stood
staring, or the old man who paused to cast
back a startled eye, "I don't know what is
wrong. I don't ask. I only tell you my be-
lief in you isn't changed. And as to my love
—that is more yours than ever because you
are troubled and forsaken."

X

ELIZABETH'S eyes turned with vague incredulity upon Wade. She seemed to take
in with a certain dimness of comprehension the details of his presence—the loung-
ing shoulders, cropped mustache, kind eyes,
straight hair.

" You don't know," she half whispered
—" you don't know about me ?"

" I know you are good, and that I love
you. That's enough."

" Oh," she murmured, cringing, " tell him,
Gracie—tell him !" She broke away from
him, and in another instant he heard her
swift, light steps on the stair.

Wade's questioning face turned upon the
little dancer.

Grace drew a sobbing breath. "It was
me," she cried, faintly. " I did it. I
blurted the whole thing right out. You see
it was this way : Bailey told me all about it

last night—it was *right* for him to tell me,
because we've got things all fixed up, and
he's spoke to mom and everything — and I
wanted to see Elizabeth and tell her I *knew*,
and that I liked her better than ever and was
proud to call her my friend. And I chased
around all evening looking for her, though
Bailey, when he went back to town on the
five train, told me I better not let her know
I was on. But I haven't the sense God
gives little ducks!" cut in Gracie, weeping;
"and when I found her in this room reading all by herself I rushed in and out with
the whole business. I told her I knew everything. I went over it all, and was just beg-
ging her to tell me if *you* knew. And then
we heard something drop on the floor—
a cane, I guess—and we looked round and
there *they* stood in the door—Graham and
old Ruley. They'd heard enough. I thought
the old man would die right there. He was
calm as an icicle. He made her give him
particulars. And then he blazed off like
something mad. He went on at her like—
oh, well, you heard some of his remarks!
Hateful, narrow-minded—"

8

"Gracie!—what for?—that's what I'm trying to find out. What does he accuse her of?—the sweetest creature on this earth."

"Oh," moaned Grace, distractedly, "I forgot you hadn't heard. She's Mary Averne, Elizabeth is. They say her Juliet's something great. Bailey's seen her play. He didn't recognize her at first, though he said he was always haunted by a feeling that her face was familiar. But he never actually knew really who she was till that day on the beach when you and Graham were struggling out in the ocean. Then he said something like a mask seemed to drop from her face. She lost hold of herself for a minute. Pain is pain. Whether you're acting it or feeling it, I guess it looks pretty much alike. Anyhow, Bailey knew her—*that* quick. He remembered Mary Averne where she takes the poison and says, 'This do I drink to thee!'"

"Mary Averne!—"

"But Bailey never said a word to any one. And a couple of weeks ago he met her leading man in town—a Mr. Wilmuth. And Wilmuth told him considerable about her—

how he'd met her down here on the beach
one night, and she begged him not to give
her away. She said her father mustn't know.
And Wilmuth promised. But seeing Bailey
was onto things—why, they talked it over."

" But how—but how—"

" —Did she keep the old man in the dark ?
As far as I can make out it was mostly the
Chicago lady's idea. She thought Elizabeth
clever. She'd heard her speak little pieces
at Sunday-school entertainments. And when
the old man lost his grip with the church she
sent for Elizabeth and got her in the way
of reading round at parlor entertainments.
And some manager offered to star her in a
Western circuit. He made her good terms,
and the Chicago lady persuaded her into it.
So they fixed up that the old man wasn't to
find out what he owed his bread-and-butter
to—it seems he don't think well of the stage.
And as he got Elizabeth's letters all from
Chicago, why, he never suspected a thing
till I gave it away "— She sprang up suddenly from the arm of the leather couch on
which, during this narrative, she had support-
ed herself. People were coming back from

the beach. Aware of her disordered looks, Grace sped away ànd up the spiral staircase.

Presently after Wade came upon Graham, who motioned him aside. The young preacher looked terribly put about.

" A surprisingly unpleasant thing," he said. " You've heard? Heavens, what a blow!"

" To—"

" Oh, to all of us!—the old man's done for. He won't survive this bolt, mark me."

" Bolt!—you talk strangely. Is the mere fact of having a daughter who is an actress—"

" Oh, you take that view! Her deceiving him, I suppose, doesn't cut any figure in your judgment of the girl?"

" Asperity and dogmatism in a father excuse cowardice and stratagem in a child."

" That sounds like a sentiment in a copybook. I don't say her course was unpardonable, but I can feel for Ruley's side of it, too. She knew how he regarded that sort of thing—"

" With the ferocious illiberality he applies to everything."

" But she knew, too, how fond of her he

is. She might, at least, have talked to him on the subject of her ambitions. It would have been honester."

"She knew better than to consult him. That libellous creed of his, which accounts human nature as mere dregs and dross, would have damned her as surely for the idea as for the act. And instead of considering the poor child's 'ambitions,' you'd better remember her necessities."

"There were other means."

"This moral babble comes poorly from you, Graham — you who 'hunt the trail of policy.' She was forced to the line she undertook by every pressure of surrounding and heredity. Every quality she has she derives naturally from the man who repudiates her with such noble fury. She is perhaps only a little less dramatic than he himself, and only a little less morbidly conscientious. I don't doubt that she's been frightfully unhappy in this life she's been leading, or that she believes herself to be all that her father declared her."

"You speak with heat," said Graham. "What I'm principally engrossed with, how-

ever, is my own share in the situation. It
goes hard with me to find out these facts concerning Miss Ruley. It changes my plans;
knocks the wind out of my sails. When I
spoke apparently against her just now, it was
to get your views. It did me good to hear
you take up for her. Personally I don't care
a rap that she's been on the stage. The thing
adds a glamour to my notions of her. There's
more in her than I dreamed of. I've heard
often in the West of Mary Averne and her
promise. I've heard her beauty and genius
discussed more than once. And to think
this little, still, dove-eyed girl should be the
same woman! It's amazing, and it fasci-
nates my imagination. But it makes it out
of the question for me to marry her. The
stage and the pulpit can't mix quite so
intimately. This isn't the millennium. A
preacher's bound to respect established prej-
udices. If I walked after my desires I
should pay for the happiness with my career. I haven't power enough to grasp the
nettle of public opinion in my hand and
crush the stings out of it. So I know better
than to touch the thing—an exceeding tough

business in any case. It's rough, though—
by Heaven it is! And philosophy is a cursed
poor substitute for my sweet Bessie's cleft
little chin and big childlike eyes!"

"Poor as it is," cut in Wade, with sudden
irascibility, "you'd have had to make it serve
even if Miss Ruley had remained what you
thought her—an obscure young person, un-
stigmatized by any blemish of talent. For
she would not have married you, permit me
to say with certainty."

Graham stared.

"Upon what—upon what grounds—"

Wade regarded him quietly. And as they
faced each other in silence Graham suddenly
seemed to comprehend what the other's suggestive stillness implied. He swallowed hard,
and drew his nether lip against his teeth.

"I should like," he said in a moment—"I
should like to hurl you over that rail. It's
you, is it? ah!" Wade burst into a little
laugh.

"Don't do it, old chap!" he said. "Remember who you are, even if you forgot
whom you're addressing. The theological
verities!—you can't afford to overlook them!"

Graham turned away, and then, after a moment, wheeled back and clapped Wade's arm rather cordially, though his face was grayish.

"All right," he said. "You and I can't quarrel. I remember that hideous hour out in that stretch of sea, when—no, Wade, no! I deserve this. I'm like a dastard in battle slain with the spear he has dropped in fleeing —nasty sensation." In a moment he asked, "Is it all settled—between you two?"

"It's settled with me," smiled Wade. "The other may take time. But my life's before me!"

"Oh, that's it! She—yes, she loves you. A hundred circumstances of proof recur to me. But if you've got to win her across this breach—alas! you'll need your wit, my boy. Sweet as she is, she is narrow, too—a Calvinist at heart. You should have heard her self-accusations just now! She'll refuse to blur your purple."

"And you?" suggested Wade.

"Oh, you press me home! I shall make my farewells to Ruley forthwith. And tomorrow morning, when you come down, I shall be gone. I'd go to-night," he interpolated ironically, "only Sabbath travelling, you know — ah well!" He thrust out and clasped Wade's hand, and, having wrung it hard, turned about and left him.

XI

THE morning broke gloomily, with a pee-
vish kind of drizzle fretting against the panes,
which, as Wade glanced through them, disclosed a distorted gray world without form
or fixity. The ocean looked like a great cyl-
inder of zinc. Its rising convexity was un-
marked of any object except the black shark-
shape of a barge driving to leeward. Even
the *Lizzie' B*—the little pleasure-yacht always
to be seen off the bar of mornings and nights
—seemed to have scudded out of reach of a
threatening storm. The streets were drenched
to an ochreous hue, and every passing omni-
bus was loaded with people for whom the
end of the season had been hastened by re-
ports of a big rainfall.

Things in the lower part of the Dorsheimer
Arms were cheerless enough to account for
any number of rapid departures. Over it
hung the dreariness peculiar in time of foul

weather to houses built for summer and sunshine; and guests who were not paying bills
and otherwise preparing to take leave stood
about desolately, making little effort at occu-
pation. A party of elderly women in the
parlor were playing a sober game of cards.
A child, unoppressed by the general atmosphere, beat with a fist upon the keys of an
aged piano which lingered ingloriously behind a door of the reading-room. The clerk,
busy and distracted, now and then threw as
polite a word as he seemed able to evoke to
the group of girls hanging about his desk.
For once mirth was notably absent from
the rooms and corridors of the Dorsheiner
Arms, and Wade, coming in from a walk on
the sodden porch, was conscious of leaving
better cheer behind him than the office afforded.

Presently his observance of the stairway
was rewarded by the appearance of two figures, at sight of which he rose at once. Elizabeth Ruley, with Miss Gayle at her elbow,
came towards him. At his look of interroga-
tion she said, hopelessly, " He will not see
me at all. I have sent to ask him. I have

gone to his door." She drew a sharp breath, adding, "He did not even speak to me." Hurrying on, she touched Wade's sleeve with a little impetuous motion of appeal. "He likes you so much!—do you think, would you be willing to—to go to him? Oh, if you could persuade him just to see me! Anything would be better for him than this! He was just so when — when his other trouble came upon him—the church trouble. He shut himself up, and we could not tell how he was taking it or what he might do."

"I will do anything you advise," said Wade, feeling his throat ache at sight of her drawn little face and shadowed eyes. "Sit here while I go and see what can be done."

He left her in the reading-room, and went away and sent up to Mr. Ruley a formal request to speak with him; but the bell-boy who carried the message returned to say that Mr. Ruley was unable to see any one. Obliged to carry this information to the young woman in the reading-room, Wade had the further discomfort of seeing her deeply cast down by the failure of her plan. Her head dropped despairingly against the worn leather of the long couch-pillow, and her hands twisted together in an extremity of anguish.

"I deserve it," she breathed. "He is just, only just, my father, in casting me off like this. I did not want to ask his forgiveness. I cannot ever hope for that. But there are many ways in which he needs me: I must help him dress, I must fix the beef-tea for him, and take his breakfast up. I only want to beg him to let me serve him in the old way. But I am not fit even for that!"

"Elizabeth!" cried Wade, "don't blame yourself like this!"

"I can never blame myself enough. I want to tell him that I haven't waited till now for punishment. I've had it right along—daily, hourly. I never threw myself so completely into any character but that I was conscious of my own guilt and danger, and wondering if there might not be in the audience that saw me some one who knew Elizabeth Ruley. When I was home at odd times in High Ripple, or anywhere with my father, I tried to make my face absolutely blank, for fear a vivid expression of any sort of thought or feeling might recall to a stranger's eye the face of Mary Averne. I locked myself in a kind of stony cell of control, and I stifled there, longing sometimes to cry out, to manifest in one way or other the poor self that was thus barred in, walled up. I have suffered — yes, I have suffered, as it was right I should; for I have sinned against everything —rearing, conviction, a daughter's duty. Oh, I realize the truth of what you want to say! —that there is nothing essentially wrong in the profession I have followed. For most women, perhaps not. For me, with my breeding and my beliefs—yes, yes!"

" But, dearest! the general truth can't be the specific falsehood, nor the abstract right the concrete wrong. Look at the thing broadly, widely. Drop a standard that is merely local and temporary. As to your father's justice, he is just perhaps, but merely according to the range of one who stands upon a dark crag of moral vision and sees only a desolated valley below him. I don't want to offend you by criticising him, Elizabeth; but it seems to me that no man is fit to judge his fellow-beings who cannot see something of the incradicable good which lies somewhere in the lowest of us."

" Lowest!" She caught at the word. " Yes, yes ; we are all corrupt, debased—"

" Oh no, we're not, Elizabeth! How your mind fastens to its traditions of a fallen race ! But it is natural that you should see only what you have been taught to see— a slavish and vicious humanity, a violent and tyrannical God. These ideas belong to each other. Change one and the other changes. See something noble in the creature—' man, whose name and nature God disdained not,' and at once an implacable and contemptuous creator becomes impossible. The work of our hands is dear to us even in its imperfections."

" I think you misunderstand my father's position. You are like the church people who tired of his teachings, and, like most folk in this time of creedal change, you prefer to the Jehovah of the Scriptures a smilingly complacent Deity, who shall find it pleasanter to be merciful than just. I have old - fashioned ideas myself. I would rather never bow the knee at all than worship a divine senti-

mentalist, always readier to weep over the
sinner than to approve the righteous. The
God of my faith holds a sword, and not a
censer. Vice cannot be perfumed away; it
must be cut off."

"Your faith, then, my dearest, is Hebraic
rather than Christian. You hold by the law
rather than the sacrifice."

"I hold by my father's God."

"A hurler of thunder-bolts, merciless, vin-
dictive—a being, indeed, singularly after your
father's own mortal plan. Have you ever noticed that our gods are wonderfully like
ourselves? The Chinese deity has oblique
eyes, the African thick lips, Zeus of the
Athenians a Greek profile. But why are
we talking of all this? I only want to make
you believe that you ought not to judge yourself so harshly. Your motives were good.
You sinned, perhaps, in deceiving him. But
sins vary; some of them have a nobler sa-
vor than the catechism taste of what is
merely moral. An unscrupulous honesty
isn't the highest good. To be willing, for
another's happiness, to sin and bear the inevitable issue of sin, seems to me some-

thing finer than the rough-shod virtue which tramples heavenward upon the sensibilities of other people."

"Oh," she murmured, "how gently you deal with—with—"

"The woman I love?" He laughed softly. In her next words she took tacit account of this murmured phrase.

"Your very generosity separates us infinitely," she said.

Wade frowned.

"My generosity?"

"Don't you see how it is?—I am the more unworthy."

"Oh, a jackstraw of a notion for me to overthrow!" He laughed again, committing the error of refusing to take her scruples seriously. "But can't you see, dear, that you are encouraging vice when you use a man's virtues against him? When you are my wife—"

"A woman whose father discards her isn't fit to be—your wife."

"I care nothing for—"

"*I* care. From my father's hand or—not at all." She spoke steadily. He tried to detain her that he might attack this decision

9

from another point; but she went away, only looking back once over her shoulder, a little shadowy creature enough with her sorrowful eyes, but with something in her lips of her father's indomitable quality.

All day long the rain whimpered on the panes. Towards night a high wind began to whirl in from the swelling sea, whipping round the house's frail walls in great blasts. A constant thudding of shutters and an occasional crashing of insecurely set glass aggravated the clamor of the storm. When the office door was opened never so little a flawy sweep of rain lifted the papers to the ceiling. People whose summery cottons were supplemented with shawls and jackets hung about stairs and halls talking ominously of the various contingencies of a coast tempest. Tidal waves were darkly mentioned. If the roof of the Dorsheimer Arms stayed over it every one would be surprised. An air of foreboding pervaded the gloomy wastes of rooms, deepening as the blast screamed still more shrilly, and the electric lamps, sickening to mere scarlet threads in their crystal lobes, finally shuddered out, and left to the

jaundiced rays of a few hastily-lighted gas-
jets the scared faces of the women grouped
anxiously about.

"Mom is like she was crazy," said Grace
Gayle to Wade, over the baluster. "She
hears banshees and things keening under the
window. Between her and Elizabeth I've got
my hands full." She looked, indeed, far less
smart than her wont. Her hair was uncurled,
and fell around her common little features in
masses much softer than usual. "This is
beef-tea," she pursued, indicating the covered
cup she carried, "for *him*."

"Mr. Ruley?"

"Mm. Elizabeth's promised to go to bed
in case I can get this delivered into his own
hands. She says he's used to having it this
time every night. The bell-boys are mostly
busy just now holding down the roof—anyhow, I don't see 'em about. So I'm going to
beard the lion myself."

"Can't I take it?"

"I guess I'll try it myself," she decided.
"I oughtn't to shirk anything, for I feel awful
guilty about this whole business. Oh, if
Bailey was only here!"

"Bailey!—oh, I'd forgotten. The real thing, is it, Gracie?"

"You can put your last cent on it," said Gracie, solemnly; "I wouldn't be going to marry him if it wasn't. Oh, I'm struck!—but we're going slow — very slow. This world-without-end business ought not to be rushed. If I haven't got the everlasting and eternal kind of love you read about, I want to know it before I get over my depth. That's what I told Bailey—that I have to have a long, long time to think it over. We're both awful serious—no mad haste or other foolishness about us. Of course, man-*like*, Bailey would have liked it better if I'd demanded less time, but he finally agreed with me that time was the only thing to judge constancy by. So we're going to wait six weeks." Smiling gravely she went on up-stairs.

Laying her knuckles against Mr. Ruley's door she held herself to listen. At the second knock the slow and steady sound of pacing feet within the room ceased, and a voice said, "Well?"

"Your beef-tea," replied Gracie, assuming a boyish intonation.

"'THIS IS BEEF-TEA FOR *HIM*'"

"None to-night, thank you."

"Please, sir—"

"Well?"

"I got to obey orders. They told me to leave it." There was a kind of murmur from behind the dark panels. Then the key clicked, and Mr. Ruley's face showed in a narrow opening of the door.

It was so stern—that stony-looking face with its hollow, feverish eyes and tufts of brows and frayed ends of rumpled hair—that Gracie uttered a little gasp of alarm. Mr. Ruley stared distantly at her and his long nostrils dilated. He made a sudden movement as if to shut the door again, but Grace put herself in the way.

"Woman," began Mr. Ruley, sternly. Gracie's blood rose.

"Bear in mind that I'm not your daughter. You can't call me names. I've never taken abuse from any one, and I won't from you! Here's your beef-tea. I guess it ain't very hot, but I had trouble enough to get it as it is. But Elizabeth—"

"I refuse to hear any more."

"Unless you're going to shut the door on

my hand, you'll have to. I'm not afraid of you—I have been, but I'm not now. I don't respect you enough to be afraid. No, not if you *are* a preacher!—a preacher!" she repeated in an accent of irony, " why, if you were the One you preach about you couldn't set yourself up any higher! For even *He* isn't too holy to forgive folks that slip up once and again, and *you* are. Your own flesh and blood, too! That makes it worse. It isn't because Elizabeth has sinned against God that you carry on like this, and won't speak to her and starve yourself to death, and have folks trailing across a wet court-yard to make you beef-tea in a big empty kitchen where there's mice running around —it's because she's sinned against *you*. It isn't piety that's got you—it's pride. That's all I got to say. I didn't expect to open my mouth. I didn't dream I'd dare to. And I got a queer, shaky feeling in my hands this minute. Take this cup, quick!"

Gasping a little with excitement, she thrust the cup into his hand and turned away. Half-way down the corridor she glanced back. The door of Mr. Ruley's room was still open, and

Mr. Ruley himself, drawn to some petrifaction of anger or amazement, stood rooted in the space. His eyes were fixed upon her own retreating figure. The storm within seemed to render him unaware of the clash and roar of the storm without.

"Oh, he's awful!" sighed Grace, aghast to remember what she had said to the old man.

After midnight the wind seemed somewhat to abate. People timorously sought their beds, and Wade presently went also to his room. It was still very early in the morning when he woke to find a dawn of dazzling primrose unfolding in the storm-free sky. But, though it was yet barely day, a crowd appeared to be gathering on the beach, and, observing the hurrying midge-like figures to the left of the upper board walk, Wade decided that perhaps the life-saving station had been called to service by some disabled ship off the bar.

He dashed into his clothes. The halls looked dark. No one was stirring, but as the young man turned the stair's first landing he saw a figure laboriously coming along the passage below.

It took Wade another glance to determine the shuffling form as that of Mr. Ruley. The old preacher fingered the wall as he advanced, and a ray of amber light striking through a window at the end of the hall gave his face an unearthly kind of glow. His very garments had that air of laxity and unfitness which a dead man's attire sometimes shows in accommodating itself to stiff limbs. But it was his expression rather than any details of his garb or gait which gave Wade a sense of chill.

His gaze was very gentle, but its mildness bore to the young man's mind no intimation of benignity. It was hardly a spiritual conformation at all, but more like a passive fleshly mood, as if the spiritual had gone or had utterly given over control of the body.

"Is it you?" he said to Wade. "I—was looking for some one—"

" Your daughter?" suggested Wade, as the old man fastened upon his strength with a kind of clinging satisfaction.

" My daughter?—yes. Yes, I believe so. I wanted some one. It is not good for so old a man to be left alone." He had turned, and was guiding Wade down the passage. On the threshold of his room a few scraps of broken china lay.

"I dropped it," he said. "The cup she brought me—the dancing-girl."

"Gracie?"

"I believe so. She spoke to me—of many things. I cannot recall them ; of Elizabeth—the child of my old age—a repentant sinner. I should like to recall what she said, but it's been so long now, I—I can't. I have suffered much. But it is God's great tenderness, His unceasing—unceasing love that leaves my faculties clear and—and strong through all this stress. In green pastures—and by still waters—but I was speaking of the dancing-girl—not Salome—this other one. The mighty fall. And through His loving-kindness the weak things of this world—the weak things prevail. He prepareth a table for me—He prepareth—a table—" He rambled on through an incoherency of scriptural allusion, referring often to his daughter, and rubbing his hands ceaselessly together as he sat on the bedside and smiled vaguely, and sometimes left off smiling to pluck soberly at a ray of sunshine flickering over his knee.

Under the dim abstraction of those peaceful eyes Wade's heart faltered to an aghast conviction of all that their roving glances meant. He had taken his last hurt, had Mr. Ruley. The tension had been too much for the mental fabric. If it had not snapped wholly asunder, at least its power had lost all elasticity. It had not rebounded from this final jerk of fate, but had settled to a sort of senile flaccidity.

"In the fulness of my years—a ripened shock—my dear one, my Bessie, is with me to—" The old man paused, with his mild gaze on the door. The knob had seemed to turn a little from the outside, as if in an experimentative hand. It clicked back as the door sprung open, revealing Elizabeth herself in the hall. Her eyes went wide at sight of Wade. Something like joy leaped to her face as she bent a swift gaze on her father and saw his placidity of brow. It seemed to flash upon her that this unexpected mildness of feature was in some sort due to the young man—that he, perhaps, had mediated for her.

"Oh," she cried, "*you*, you have done this!" And, clasping her father, she sobbed, "You forgive me, then!—and *he* has brought it about! Oh, I'm glad it was he!" Mr. Ruley's countenance exhibited a struggling comprehension.

"Our young friend, Mr. Wade?" he asked. "Yes, I remember not long since when I— I—you had done something to offend me —he upheld you—I remember it all very well." He stroked his daughter's hair as he spoke, but something in his words or manner startled her. She drew back. The vacant amiability in the old man's regard of her appeared to strike her to the soul. She turned almost wildly to Wade.

"What is it?" she breathed. "Doesn't he *know* me? Oh—"

"Know you?" repeated Mr. Ruley, with gentle reproach. "Certainly. Though you grow so tall, Bessie! and your long curls?— cut off—all cut off—mm! A pity!" She rose. She seemed about to fall, and Wade, rising also, drew her face upon his shoulder. In that moment of utter weakness and desperate realization she had no objections, no scruples, no provisions against the love she had been able in lesser straits to renounce. She merely clung to Wade, speechlessly, blindly.

"A good child," murmured the old man, with an eye of remote approval. "'Sweet is thy voice and thy countenance is comely.'" His face clouded a little. "You will be kind to her?" he asked Wade, with a kind of doubt. "If I remember well I have sometimes been severe, somewhat severe, with this cherished daughter of mine. But I thought I was right."

"Father, you *were* right!"

"I believe I was," quavered Mr. Rulcy, brightening up. "I executed justice. I was right. But," he added, in a mildly querulous fashion, "what difference does it make, anyway?"

The sun was shining now with blinding radiance. White-caps danced along the sea, which, still upheaved, flashed like a dolphin's back scaled with silver. Among the loose and shattered timber of the ocean walk throngs were gathering, discussing the ravages of the storm, laughing, chattering as gayly as ever. Everything wore a jocund as-

pect, a cheeriness such as hangs upon the
subsidence of peril or disaster. The tempest had passed, and it was well with the
blithe summer city.

But beached below the last pavilion a
wrecked vessel lay black and crushed, with a
shattered mast lunging across it into the
sand. It spoke a mute tale of stress and anguish and stifled prayers and futile effort. It
was tragic enough; yet children clambered
over it, shouting joyously, incoming waves
wreathed it with blossomy white, and here
and there wet patches of the battered hulk
mirrored what it had never rendered back
while it stoutly rode the seas—little glimpses
of the blue sky that shines over all mortal
things.

THE END